Hemispheric Trade and Economic Integration After NAFTA

Proceedings of the Indianapolis Summit December 6-7, 1994

Edited by Richard Starr,
Research Fellow
The Competitiveness Center
of Hudson Institute

The Competitiveness Centre of Hudson Institute
Indianapolis, Indiana
and
The Fraser Institute
Vancouver, British Columbia

The Fraser Institute thanks the **Lilly Endowment Inc. of Indianapolis** for their generous funding of this project.

The Indianapolis Summit was sponsored by **The Fraser Institute** and **The Competitiveness Center of Hudson Institute** and was co-hosted by: American Enterprise Institute; Atlas Economic Research Foundation; The Brookings Institution; Centro de Estudios Publicos; Centro de Investigaciones Sobre la Libre Empresa; Columbus Group; Fundacion Libertad; Fundacion Republica; Institute for International Economics; and Instituto Libertad y Desarrollo.

Printed in Canada.

Canadian Cataloguing in Publication Data

Indianapolis Summit (1994)
Hemispheric trade and economic integration after NAFTA

ISBN 0-88975-151-X

1. Western hemisphere—Economic integration—Congresses.
2. North America—Economic integration—Congresses. 3.
South America—Economic integration—Congresses. 4.
Foreign trade regulation—Congresses.   I. Starr, Richard,
1961-   II. Fraser Institute (Vancouver, B.C.)   III. Title.
HF1745.152 1995   382'.917   C95-910332-5

Table of Contents

Introduction
Thomas J. Duesterberg 1

The Future of Hemispheric Free Trade
Congressman Lee Hamilton 11

Session 1 :   The NAFTA Treaty and the Question of Expansion:
              Views of the Negotiators
Julius Katz 23
John Weekes 31

Session 2:   Economic Benefits of NAFTA and Hemispheric Integration
Alan Reynolds 41
Riordan Roett 47
Roberto Salinas-Léon 53
Sidney Weintraub 65

Democracy and Free Trade in the Western Hemisphere
Senator Richard Lugar 71

Session 3:   Next Steps in Expanding NAFTA and Building Hemispheric
              Economic Integration: The View from Canada and the U.S.
David Malpass 85
Jeffrey Schott 91
Ronald J. Wonnacott 97

Session 4:   Next Steps in Expanding NAFTA and Building Hemispheric
              Economic Integration: The View from Latin America
Congressman José María Ibarbia 111
Cristían Larroulet 125
Luis-Hernan Paul 151

The Economic Integration of Our Hemisphere
Ambassador Everett Ellis Briggs 159

Stability and Security—Keys to Enhanced Trade in Latin America
Ambassador Jon Glassman 167

Session 5:   Economic Integration: International Perspectives from the Media
David Asman 183
Howard Banks 191
Peter Cook 195

Session 6:   Next Steps in the Business Community in Shaping and Promoting
              Economic Integration in the Hemisphere
Harry Freeman 199
Victor Garcia Laredo 207
Timothy Page 217

Introduction: The Promise of Hemispheric Economic Integration— the 1994 Summit and Beyond

THOMAS J. DUESTERBERG

I. Background: The Historic Opportunity for Hemispheric Integration

In 1967, President Lyndon Johnson attended the last formal summit of heads of state from the Western Hemisphere, which was held in Punta del Este. The signature policy achievement of that meeting was the commitment of Latin American nations, fully supported by the U.S., to build a "common market" for trade and economic cooperation. President Johnson stated to his counterparts at the summit: "...you will be forging a great new common market—expanding your industrial base, increasing your participation in world trade, and broadening economic opportunity. I have already made my position clear to my Congress and my people: If Latin America decides to create a common market, I shall recommend a substantial contribution to a fund that would help ease the transition into an integrated regional economy."

The solemn commitment taken in 1967 quickly faded into inaction and disillusionment; national economies retreated into autarky behind high tariff barriers, and the standard of living in much of Latin American soon entered a period of long decline. Tension and

---

Thomas J. Duesterberg is Director of the Competitiveness Center of Hudson Institute.

misunderstanding between North and South replaced the hope of the Alliance for Progress.

Now, 27 years later, the heads of state of 34 nations of the Western Hemisphere have met again. In Miami on December 9-10, they set out an ambitious agenda of economic integration. A great deal has changed since 1967, most notably the fact that nearly every country in the hemisphere is governed by some form of democracy, with the obvious exception of Cuba, which was not represented in Miami. The combination of democratization, increasing openness to global economic integration, and more effective domestic economic strategies has set the stage for greater optimism about achieving the objectives laid out in Miami in late 1994.

Political and economic conditions in much of Latin America have changed dramatically since 1967, making it now possible to improve economic well being throughout the hemisphere and build closer political ties grounded in mutual interest between North and South. The single most important change has been the remarkable shift toward free market economics and democracy since the mid-1980s. Perhaps the most dramatic shift was in Mexico. Faced with economic stagnation and a crisis of confidence in both the economy and government, Mexico began to shed a century-old policy of protecting domestic markets and directing the economy from Mexico City. In its place have come deregulation, privatization of industry and services, free trade and deepening of democratic institutions. Mexico's new openness, symbolized by the North American Free Trade Agreement (NAFTA), exposes its developing industries, financial markets and service providers to competition from Canada and the U.S. The results have been impressive. The Mexican economy produced strong and consistent growth from 1986 through 1994, reversed the flow of capital out of the country, and increased per capita income. Despite a setback at the end of 1994 due to difficulties in managing a substantial imbalance in the current account and the steady globalization of capital markets, Mexico's leaders remain committed to the economic strategies that set the stage for sustainable growth and led to NAFTA.

Mexico has also built a network of free trade ties to other Latin American countries, and its example of economic decentralization and free trade has proven successful enough to merit broad imitation. Chile had started on a similar path almost 20 years ago and is enjoying consistent growth of 6–7 percent annually. Colombia, Venezuela, Peru, Argentina and other countries followed suit as the Mexican and Chilean models proved successful. Even Brazil, long accustomed to a state-directed economy and leadership in the non-aligned movement, has recognized the success of its neighbors and is beginning to decentralize its huge economy and adopt freer trade policies. Growth in 1994 in Brazil, Argentina and Chile, which represent 80 percent of the economy of South America, will average 6 percent as a result of the new economic policies. Bear Stearns analyst David Malpass argues that the southern cone of the region is creating "a new world growth hub to compete with North America and China."

In addition to the NAFTA accord, an increasingly complex web of bilateral and sub-regional trade agreements have sprung up or been revitalized to link Latin American economies in free trade areas or through reductions in barriers to trade and investment. Central America, the Andean region, the Southern cone (Mercosur), and the Caribbean have all set up sub-regional agreements. Mexico has free trade agreements with Colombia and Venezuela and with Central American nations. In 1985, average import tariffs in Latin America were among the highest in the world, at about 56 percent on a trade weighted basis. By mid-1992, the average was down to 16 percent and is now even lower due to the combined effects of the Uruguay Round and the various regional agreements.

As a result of falling trade barriers and renewed growth, trade in the Western Hemisphere has doubled in the last 10 years. Foreign direct investment in Latin America has soared from negative numbers in the mid '80s to over $21 billion in 1994. Net capital flows into the region rose from $25 billion to $69 billion between 1990 and 1993.

The economic dynamism and move to free trade in Latin America has also proven quite beneficial to the U.S. economy, primarily because the U.S. has long been the region's supplier of choice, controlling over one-half of its export market. In the last 10 years, U.S. exports of goods to Latin America have grown by over 350 percent. The U.S. now sells 70 percent more in terms of goods to

Latin America than to Japan and nearly as much as to all of the European Union. The U.S. in 1994 will sell over $88 billion in goods and $28 billion in services to Latin America and will have a net trade surplus of around $10 billion with the region. The NAFTA accord has helped increase U.S. exports to Mexico by 18 percent to almost $50 billion in 1994, and will create over 100,000 new American jobs this year alone for U.S. suppliers of goods. Around 10,000 U.S. workers, on the other hand, have been displaced this year by new competition from Mexico.

Canada, too, has benefited from NAFTA. Since the trade pact went into effect, Canadian exports to Mexico have jumped by 33 percent and Canadian exports to the U.S. have risen 20 percent. Canadian trade with the U.S. is up 45 percent since passage of the U.S.-Canadian Free Trade Agreement in 1989. The Canadian economy is one of the fastest growing in the entire industrialized world due in large part to the rapid pace of export growth.

This rapid pace of intra-regional growth in trade and capital flows will temporarily slow due to the devaluation of the Mexican peso at the end of 1994. Nonetheless, the long term growth prospects remain solid. According to estimates of the Office of the U.S. Trade Representative, the U.S. will be selling over $250 billion in goods to Latin America by the year 2010, dwarfing the estimated $128 billion in sales to Europe and $88 billion to Japan. U.S. trade with Latin America in 1994 has already grown at more than twice the rate of overall trade and 70 percent faster than trade with East Asia, the other rapidly growing region of the world.

Such economic dynamism has helped nurture political decentralization throughout Latin America, as deregulation, privatization and individual enterprise have proven much more compatible with democratic than authoritarian forms of government. Reducing the regulatory role of government through elimination of trade barriers and privatization leaves less room, by definition, for government control over society, spurring democracy and greater local or individual empowerment. Even in times of crisis, such as in Chile in the early 1980s and in Mexico at the end of 1994, democratic forces have held firm and sustained the market liberalization policies which had been put in place.

Recognizing this connection, the Bush Administration had encouraged Latin American nations on the path of reform with the 1990 Enterprise for the Americas Initiative (EAI), which in some respects reformulated the 1967 vision of a common market into one of a hemispheric free trade area to include the U.S. and Canada. EAI implicitly offered permanent access to the U.S. market and debt reduction, as Latin American countries adapted market oriented and fiscally conservative economic policies and broadened their democratic institutions.

Now, the advanced economies of Latin America such as Chile, Argentina and Colombia, are determined to follow the lead of Mexico and join NAFTA. Gaining permanent access to the large North American market would help sustain momentum for their own trade liberalization measures and help strengthen the legitimacy of their democracies.

Despite the apparent momentum for further economic integration in the hemisphere, a number of developments in the last two years led to doubts about achieving the historic opportunity for closer economic ties. For example, early in the Clinton administration, the decision was made to end the EAI, which had been so well accepted in Latin America. The new U.S. administration frequently confused the message of economic cooperation by trying to weave programs of "sustainable development," environmental protection, worker rights and institution building, which often appear patronizing to Latin Americans, into the economic policy fabric. Moreover, until the pressure of the Miami Summit forced a policy reversal, the Clinton administration failed to provide any solid commitment to grant Chile's request for a free trade agreement. The U.S. also was unable to provide any NAFTA-equalization benefits to the Caribbean countries, and even failed to preserve its ability to negotiate new trade agreements under the so-called fast track authority.

While attention to a variety of concerns is constructive to a mature dialogue, doubts about the U.S. ability to deliver on the promise of free trade and economic integration caused its hemispheric trading partners to be suspicious of U.S. intentions and critical of U.S. leadership. Canadian trade minister Roy McLaren stated: "After urging the vision of free trade from Alaska to Tierra del Fuego, the

U.S. appears to have lost its momentum." He suggested that Latin countries begin to reevaluate their options and consider bilateral deals with Canada, Mexico, and even nations in Europe and Asia if hemispheric free trade appeared low on the list of U.S. priorities. The *Washington Post* recently reported that some Canadian leaders would even consider abrogating NAFTA due to U.S. affronts over trade and apparent lack of conviction in pursuing hemispheric integration.

Chile is already exploring options for more trade with Argentina and Brazil, a reversal of their traditional antipathy toward these larger neighbors. Argentina has begun sending signals that the ambiguous U.S. policy is causing it to look to the southern cone and to Europe for new opportunities. Brazil has always been suspicious of U.S. domination and appears to be trying to draw Chile and Argentina closer to a South American strategy as an alternative to NAFTA accession. At a summit in Essen in mid-December 1994, the European Union decided to open exploratory talks with Mercosur about trade liberalization between the two regions, giving some credence to Brazilian attempts to provide an alternative to NAFTA accession.

Other factors were also at work to dull the impetus for closer hemispheric ties. U.S. political intervention in the Caribbean and lingering immigration problems have caused friction. Mexico is chafing at the passage of Proposition 187 in California. Central American and Caribbean nations complain of a reduction in U.S. development assistance, lack of preferential access to the NAFTA economic zone, and heavy-handed U.S. intervention in the region. The U.S. also continues to impose irritating trade restrictions on Latin American exports such as cut flowers, tuna, textiles, cement, sugar, and other indigenous products. Protectionist forces in the U.S. will undoubtedly seize on the Mexican peso crisis to renew their attacks on the NAFTA agreement itself.

On the Latin American side, too, recent events have clouded the most optimistic scenarios for uninterrupted growth, democratization, and opening to the outside. Venezuela, Brazil, Colombia and Peru have had both economic and political setbacks which shook confidence in their commitment to liberalization. Mexico in 1994 experienced both political unrest and financial instability which shook the confidence of international investors.

Fortunately, the political commitment to economic integration from both North and South was sufficiently strong to insure a good result at the Miami summit. Responding to the strong push by Argentina, Chile, Canada and others, the 34 leaders assembled in Miami pledged to complete a "Free Trade Area of the Americas" (FTAA) by 2005. Work is to begin immediately on harmonizing existing regional agreements as a prelude to the FTAA. Chile was invited to join the NAFTA, and negotiations are to begin in spring 1995. The three NAFTA signatories will begin immediately to draft a common set of criteria to assess eligibility of other nations to join NAFTA. Commitments were made to facilitate investment flows throughout the region. Finally, the U.S. pledged to continue working with Congress to meet the concerns of Caribbean nations likely to be hurt by trade and investment diversion due to NAFTA. Thus, the results of the Miami Summit have raised expectations even higher than those flowing from the Punta del Este Summit of 1967.

II. The Indianapolis Summit

The Indianapolis Summit was conceived as an effort to draw attention to and build support for continuing the process of hemispheric economic integration. Sponsored by the Fraser Institute and Hudson Institute, the Indianapolis Summit was held on December 6 and 7, 1994, just days prior to the summit in Miami. It was co-hosted by a number of distinguished research institutions and business organizations from North and South America, and intended to show the broad base of support for more rapid economic integration. The speakers represented a broad cross section of business, political and opinion leaders throughout the hemisphere, united only by general support for continued economic integration.

Institutions and organizations which co-hosted the Indianapolis Summit included: the American Enterprise Institute, the Atlas Economic Research Foundation, the Brookings Institution, the Centro de Estudios Publicos (Chile), the Centro de Investigaciones Sobre la Libre Empresa (Mexico), the Columbus Group (Mercosur region), the Fundacion Libertad (Argentina), the Fundacion Republica (Argentina), the Institute for International Economics, and the Instituto Libertad y Desarrollo (Chile).

The papers from that meeting which are collected here naturally reflect uncertainty regarding the final outcome of the Miami Summit. Given the doubts about the eventual outcome of the Miami Summit and the importance of taking advantage of the historic opportunity for hemispheric progress in late 1994, the two conference organizers felt that a program supporting the general theme of economic integration would be timely and useful. Additionally, we thought that collecting a group of documents from this conference would be helpful to making the case for economic integration in coming months and years. Even with the strong political statement of intention that was taken in Miami, the experience of the 1967 Summit and subsequent developments are ample evidence of the need for organizing support for implementation of the political commitment. Additionally, the year-end financial crisis in Mexico again cast some doubt on the logic of integration throughout the hemisphere. This collection, then, is intended to provide an easily accessible and coherent group of papers reviewing the economic, political and historical impetus for hemispheric economic integration.

The papers in this collection show lively disagreement on many points. But they share a common grounding of expertise in the history of, and economic rationale for, hemispheric integration, and a commitment to trade liberalization in one form or another. Although most of the speakers cut across normal academic disciplines in their papers, they fall into five general categories.

First, political leaders from North and South America included Senator Richard Lugar, Congressman Lee Hamilton, and Congressman José María Ibarbia. This group reviewed the political and diplomatic impetus for closer hemispheric economic ties. It is clear from the papers of this bipartisan and international group that a good deal of political capital has been invested in hemispheric integration, even through some caution about the timetable for achieving it was evident.

Second, a group of economists or political economists, including Roberto Salinas, Cristián Larroulet, Ronald Wonnacott, Alan Reynolds, Sidney Weintraub, Jeffrey Schott, David Malpass, Riordan Roett and Luis-Hernan Paul, reviewed the economic justification for trade liberalization. Their papers often covered both a review of the impact of free trade agreements already in place in the hemisphere and projections of the effects of further liberalization. It is worth noting that most of these papers were prepared prior to the late-December devaluation of the Mexican peso, and so do not take into account the short-run impact of this event.

Third, several present or former government officials reviewed the record of free trade negotiations for helpful lessons about the future as well as insights about the original intentions of NAFTA participants for eventual expansion of that agreement. This group included Julius Katz and John Weekes. Former Ambassador Jon Glassman also placed trade agreements between North and South in the larger context of U.S.-Latin American relations.

Fourth, representatives of the business community provided insights into the support of business throughout the hemisphere for free trade, as well as some realistic comments on the political feasibility of further expansion of free trade. This group included Victor Garcia Laredo, Harry Freeman, Timothy Page and Ambassador Everett Ellis Briggs. Finally, a group of journalists from North America commented on the state of public debate about free trade and the likely prospects for both press and general public support of further free trade agreements. This group included David Asman, Howard Banks and Peter Cook.

This volume, then, brings together papers by a diverse group of experts commenting on the need for and the likelihood of achieving the vision of the FTAA. While any attempt to summarize their views would do an injustice to the richness and diversity of their arguments, a few common themes do emerge. Simply put, these are the economic and political imperative for continuing to seek hemispheric integration, and the need to move quickly to seize the historic window of opportunity that now exists for accomplishing such an ambitious goal.

The Future of Hemispheric Free Trade

CONGRESSMAN LEE H. HAMILTON

I want to congratulate the Hudson and Fraser Institutes for putting together a fascinating agenda and for assembling an impressive group of specialists to discuss it. Hudson and Fraser also deserve praise for their contributions to the public debate on NAFTA and other hemispheric issues during the past couple of years. I am especially pleased that an institution in my home state has assumed a leading role in advocating closer ties in the Western Hemisphere. We are accustomed to hearing pleas for the hemisphere from institutions in Florida and the border states, but we rarely hear about these issues from the Midwest. That makes Hudson's work particularly important both in Washington and in the Midwest.

Introduction

A conference on trade and the Western Hemisphere could not be held at a more opportune time. The House's and the Senate's overwhelming approval of the Uruguay Round has generated optimism about bipartisan support for free trade. And this weekend President Clinton will host a summit meeting of hemispheric leaders in

---

Representative Lee Hamilton has served Indiana's Ninth Congressional District since January 1965. He is Indiana's senior member in the House of Representatives and former Chairman of the House Committee on Foreign Affairs.

Miami, who hope to inaugurate an era of closer economic and political cooperation.

This morning I want to address several issues relating to these two important events:

- First, NAFTA, which paved the way for the Miami Summit.

- Second, the Summit's importance.

- Third, the prospects for free trade in the hemisphere.

- Fourth, trade politics in the United States.

- Finally, the key trade policy challenges of the next Congress and the coming decade.

NAFTA Progress Report

Nothing will affect the prospects for hemispheric trade more profoundly than will perceptions of how NAFTA is doing. That is why we need to keep close tabs on NAFTA in the coming years, and to do whatever we can to ensure its success. So how is NAFTA doing? One year into its existence, I think it is fair to say NAFTA is doing well. Economically, NAFTA is fulfilling many of the expectations of its supporters. Politically and diplomatically, NAFTA has proven valuable in ways none of us could have predicted.

Let's look at the economic side first.

Trade with our NAFTA partners is booming. U.S. exports to Mexico were 18 percent higher in the first ten months of 1994 than they were during the same period in 1993. U.S. exports to Canada are up 10 percent. If present trends continue, increased trade with Mexico and Canada should generate a net gain of about 100,000 jobs this year. The industries experiencing the biggest export gains are among those that offer better-paying, high-skilled jobs such as autos, industrial and agricultural machinery, computers and semiconductors.

NAFTA is already influencing production and marketing plans throughout the continent. That will provide a foundation for substantial future gains. A survey of 1,000 major corporations earlier this year found that 40 percent were exploring new business opportunities in Mexico and 26 percent were planning some kind of alliance with a Mexican firm.

Indiana's economy is also benefiting in NAFTA's first year. Our exports to Mexico are 20 percent higher than last year. Large export gains have occurred in industrial machinery, computer equipment, electronic equipment, fabricated metal products, minerals, and transportation equipment.

Although the good economic news outweighs the bad, NAFTA has experienced some growing pains in its first year. U.S. imports from Mexico have outstripped U.S. exports. During the first ten months of this year the Labor Department certified 12,000 people for assistance on the grounds that their jobs were lost due to NAFTA. And in Mexico, NAFTA is making some inefficient farms, factories, and stores struggle.

Many of us here are confident freer trade with Mexico will generate net gains in employment and wages. But some of those gains may take years to materialize. In the meantime, we must make a persistent case for NAFTA. If we do not, the prospects for wider free trade will suffer.

NAFTA's Political Impact

What about NAFTA's political impact? In ways we did not expect, NAFTA has proven a bulwark of stability and a stimulus to political reform.

A rebel uprising and the assassination of a leading presidential candidate would have challenged any government. Mexico's government navigated through these tumultuous events well. The government made no wrong moves on the economy early in the year. Skilled management prevented major declines both in the stock market and in the value of the peso. The government also handled the negotiations in Chiapas capably, ending the uprising.

NAFTA—and the closer bilateral relationship it has generated—helped Mexico get through a tough year. The stability of Mexico's economy and capital flows was reinforced by the investor confidence created by NAFTA. Two U.S.-backed stand-by financing packages helped shore up the peso. Concern about how the United States might react probably restrained the government's response to the Chiapas uprising.

NAFTA also promoted political reform in Mexico. The international scrutiny generated by NAFTA helped make last August's presidential election the cleanest in many years. That gives the new Zedillo government unprecedented legitimacy, which bodes well for economic progress and reform.

NAFTA's Implementation

How is the implementation of NAFTA proceeding? In two key respects, the agreement is on track. First, Mexico' political violence did not affect NAFTA implementation. Second, NAFTA's institutional apparatus is under construction.

Implementation has been a little bumpy. There has been some chaos at the border because Mexico has been slow to make certain regulatory and customs adjustments. But U.S. trade officials say Mexico is making a good faith effort to implement NAFTA. Many early difficulties have been ironed out, and talks on accelerated tariff reductions are proceeding.

Summit of the Americas

This weekend's Americas Summit is a special event, and it is filled with potential. The summit is special for several reasons. First, it will be big. It will be the largest-ever gathering of hemispheric leaders. Second, it will be inclusive. The two preceding post-war summits excluded either Canada or portions of the Caribbean. Third, it will be extraordinarily democratic. Thirty-four democracies will be represented in Miami. No other regional gathering in the world today could boast such a total.

The Promise of Hemispheric Free Trade

The Summit's great potential comes from the remarkable convergence of thinking in the hemisphere on the need for market-oriented reform and stronger democratic institutions.

Countries throughout the hemisphere are discarding statist economic policies and opening markets to foreign commerce. The return of growth and the decline of inflation have given new democratic governments breathing space. The consensus on economic policy and democracy creates an opportunity to expand free trade—the key item on the Summit agenda.

Why is hemispheric free trade important? For Latin America, participating in a free-trade system with the United States means:

- Better access to the world's largest market, which would reward painful economic reforms.

- Increased investor confidence, which would stimulate domestic and foreign investment.

- Closer diplomatic ties with the United States and with each other, based upon a shared stake in a more prosperous regional economy.

For the United States, a hemispheric free-trade system offers:
- Privileged access to export markets with vast growth potential and a strong preference for U.S. goods.

- An effective response to the regional economic strategies of our European and Japanese competitors.

- A way to reinforce democratic and free-market reform.

- A basis for closer diplomatic cooperation.

Summit Action on Trade

Barring last-minute difficulties, Summit leaders will call for the creation of an Americas Free Trade Agreement and adopt a strategy for achieving it. That strategy will call for the merging of regional trade groupings, rather than accession to NAFTA by individual countries. To highlight the U.S. commitment to free trade, President Clinton will also ask the leaders of Mexico and Canada to join him in inviting Chile into NAFTA. I applaud President Clinton for his willingness to endorse the goal of hemispheric free trade and the inclusion of Chile in NAFTA.

I believe the Summit of the Americas is an important event. I disagree with those who say the Summit will be empty of content because the President will come to the table without the fast-track authority he needs to negotiate hemispheric trade agreements.

I know Latin American governments are disappointed fast-track was derailed. I share their regret. But the idea that the Summit can't succeed without fast-track is a relic of an earlier era, when U.S. Presidents were expected to arrive at international meetings "bearing gifts." The Americas Summit is not about patronage, but rather about endorsing a mutually beneficial economic partnership. Furthermore, the President can begin consultations on regional trade at once. He won't need fast-track for awhile.

The Summit trade initiative is an important achievement for three reasons.

First, a hemispheric endorsement of free trade will symbolize a stunning shift in the policies and fortunes of Latin America. That those nations will declare their willingness to open their economies to their colossal neighbor is a powerful sign of the region's progress. Compare that to the last hemispheric summit in 1967, when the main source of suspense was the size of the foreign aid check the United States would write for Latin America.

Second, the goal of free trade will itself serve as insurance against backsliding on economic and political reform.

Third, hemispheric governments recognize the importance of establishing mechanisms for following up on summit trade commitments. The Summit's final document will lay out a schedule of meetings over the next two years that will explore initial steps to harmonize trade and investment. I look forward to working with my colleagues in Congress to make sure the United States carries out its part of the Summit trade bargain.

Trade is the 700-pound gorilla at the Summit, but it is not the only issue on the agenda. The Summit will launch nearly 20 initiatives in three broad areas:

- Prosperity—initiatives designed to promote hemispheric economic integration;

- Democracy—initiatives focusing on reinventing government and strengthening civil society; and

- Sustainable development—initiatives promoting investment in people.

Politics of Trade

What happened to fast-track? And what are its chances in the next Congress? To answer those questions, you need to look at the changing politics of trade. Fast-track became caught in a political vise this year, squeezed by two sharply opposed perspectives on the objectives of trade agreements.

On one side are "trade activists"—liberal Democrats, public interest groups, trade unions, and others who want to link great access to the U.S. market to improvements in foreign environment and labor policies, human rights, and other conditions. On the other side are "free traders"—Republicans, economists, and others who oppose linking social or economic goals to trade. Both camps are well represented in Congress. Each wanted to impose conditions on the fast-track authority that was to be included in the Uruguay Round implementing bill.

The Administration tried for several months to come up with a formula that could earn the support of a majority of members. When that proved impossible, the Administration dropped fast-track and pledged to take it up next year.

Future of Fast Track and Free Trade

Let me address the question I know is on everybody's mind at this conference: What does a Republican-majority Congress mean for fast-track and hemispheric free trade? Your luncheon speaker, my friend Dick Lugar, may be better qualified than I to answer this. But let me take a stab.

A Republican-led Congress would normally be more likely than a Democratic-led Congress to approve fast-track authority and free-trade agreements. But there is growing dissatisfaction in Congress with both. Members of Congress understand that fast-track strengthens the President's hand in trade talks. But there is widespread disenchantment with the fast-track process.

Many members don't think there is enough meaningful consultation under the current system. There is also growing discomfort with the consideration of huge and complicated trade bills under expedited procedures. The incoming Republican majority will be reluctant to approve fast-track unless the President pledges not to bring back trade agreements with environment and labor provisions.

Congressional opposition to free trade has been growing over the past few years. This assertion may seem to be contradicted by the large victory margins in last week's Uruguay Round votes. But I would caution against reading too much into the vote of a post-election, lame-duck Congress. We should not forget in how much political difficulty the Uruguay Round was only two months ago. Despite last week's vote tally, I can assure you that many members of Congress, including myself, regarded voting "yes" as the politically risky option. That partly explains why a higher percentage of non-returning members voted for the agreement than did returning members.

NAFTA, of course, was even tougher politically. The margin of victory in the House was smaller than for any major trade agreement of the past four decades.

Apprehension about Trade

Recent congressional debates reflect growing public apprehension about trade. NAFTA and the Uruguay Round had the misfortune of being considered at a time when many Americans are feeling insecure about their economic prospects. The economic change those agreements promised reinforced anxiety about trade. Given the contribution of trade to the U.S. and world economies, it is unfortunate—and potentially harmful—that trade now inspires so much concern.

This concern about trade has several sources.

First, the integration of our economy into the world economy is exposing American workers to new competitive pressures. Free trade often takes the blame. Many American see trade, especially free trade, as a threat to their job security. If you work in a shoe plant in southeastern Indiana today, you may very well owe your job to a U.S. trade barrier.

Second, the bad news on trade travels faster than the good news. Cheap imports and emigrating plants can often be linked to specific job and wage losses. But job and wage gains due to exports are not as easily identified. Free trade's opponents are more motivated than its supporters.

Third, Americans are convinced that unfair foreign trade practices are a major source of our trade deficit and the decline of our manufacturing industries.

Finally, as I noted earlier, there is growing concern about the impact of trade on social and political values. Many on the left worry about how trade affects environmental, labor, and other standards, and want to use trade leverage to achieve social and political goals. Many on the right are concerned about the impact of international trade bodies on our sovereignty.

Strengthening Support for Free Trade

To prevent long-term erosion of public support for free trade, we need to address three priorities: education, unfair trade practices, and trade adjustment assistance.

American leaders have done a poor job of educating the public on trade and its impact on our economy. Nobody is trying to reach beyond forums like this one in a sustained way. But the opponents of free trade are increasingly well organized.

The fact is, most Americans don't hear much about trade until a major agreement is up for consideration. Then they watch large corporations mount an expensive lobbying campaign and members of Congress cut last-minute deals. They can't help but gain the impression that trade is a game played in Washington for the benefit of a few.

Let me indicate some of the points I think we need to try to convey better to Americans:

- Free trade is basically a positive-sum game.

- Open markets have been a key source of our economic strength since World War II.

- Expanding trade has a net positive impact on employment and wages.

- Low-wage jobs are affected much more by automation, education, and domestic policies then by trade.

- Protectionism is costly. It imposes a hidden tax on consumers and importers.

Corporations can help counter the impression that free trade only benefits them by publicizing credible evidence of export-related job gains. An engaged President is the most valuable educator we have. President Clinton deserves credit for trying in his public remarks to educate Americans about trade and its impact on our economy.

Support for free trade also depends upon how effective our government is in combating unfair foreign trade practices and promoting U.S. exports. We should not underestimate the political importance of an effective market-opening strategy. Prying open a foreign market can produce identifiable job gains. That reassures Americans that trade benefits them. This is one reason why I support President Clinton's somewhat tougher trade strategy and the aggressive export-promotion efforts of senior officials in the Administration.

Finally, if we want to enjoy the benefits of trade, we have to help those who are adversely affected by it. The United States currently spends much less, as a fraction of GDP, on worker training and employment counseling than nearly every other OECD nation.

There is growing recognition of the need to address the structural causes of job loss and real wage decline in the lower-skilled sectors of our economy. Trade is only one factor in this equation.

But continued political support for free trade will require us to earmark a share of any assistance to workers adversely affected by trade. The Clinton Administration made good progress on a comprehensive overhaul of U.S. worker training programs in its first two years, but legislation stalled. My understanding is that a new effort may be made next year.

Trade Agenda for 1995 and Beyond

Let me wrap up with a brief survey of the trade agenda for 1995 and beyond. Early in the new Congress, I expect the President to propose an omnibus trade bill with three main components. First, the bill will includes a grant of fast-track negotiating authority that can accommodate a range of potential hemispheric trade agreements. Second, it will include an interim trade program for the nations participating in the Caribbean Basin Initiative. The purpose would be to provide parity with NAFTA benefits. Third, the bill will renew GSP—the Generalized System of Preferences, which gives certain developing country exports lower-tariff access to the U.S. market.

The fast-track issue will spark the most controversy. The key points of contention will be the duration of the authority and whether side agreements on environment, labor and other issues should or should not be required.

Agenda for Next Decade

In the next decade, American trade policymakers will need to come to terms with several critical and unresolved issues. We will need to consider how best to improve the compatibility of environmental and trade policies and how to ensure that environmental policies and regulations are not used as disguised trade barriers. We will also need to consider the extent to which repressive labor practices should be considered an unfair trade policy, and the extent to which we can improve labor practices through trade policy.

The countries signing the Uruguay Round Agreement have agreed to discuss environment and labor practices in the WTO. But we are clearly far from achieving international consensus on these issues—or even on the question of whether they are appropriate to raise in the context of trade talks.

Other trade issues we need to address in the coming decade include:

- **Competition and antitrust policies.** These need to be better coordinated within and among countries. The United States and Japan have discussed making competition policy a major focus of their next round of bilateral talks.

- **Investment policies.** The multinationalization of business makes it difficult for nations to talk about trade without simultaneously considering investment policy.

- **Subsidies.** The Uruguay Round made progress in containing some of the predatory effects of government subsidies, especially in agriculture and high-tech R&D. But competition in subsidies could intensify without additional multilateral attention.

Conclusion

In closing, I want to congratulate the Hudson and Fraser Institutes for organizing this conference. You have a fascinating agenda to work through in the next couple of days. I hope my remarks will help frame some of the issues you will discuss.

The NAFTA Treaty and the Question of Expansion: Views of the Negotiators (I)

Ambassador Julius L. Katz

We are asked at this session to present the views of the negotiators on the question of the expansion of the NAFTA. The views I
present will be those of a *former* negotiator. Needless to say, they will
be my own views and not necessarily the views of the current or past
United States Administrations.

It would be useful, I believe, to begin with some historical
background. At the outset of the NAFTA negotiations, there was no
specific plan of action with respect to the expansion of NAFTA.
Indeed, even the inclusion of Canada in the negotiations with Mexico
for a free trade agreement was not foreordained, nor was it without
some controversy in both Canada and the U.S.

Canada, it will be recalled, concluded a free trade agreement
with the U.S. on January 1, 1988. After a noisy domestic debate,
culminating in Parliamentary elections later that year, the agreement
was approved.

When it was announced in 1990 that the United States and
Mexico were contemplating negotiations for a free trade agreement,
some in the Canadian cabinet believed that Canada should seek to join
in the negotiations. Their reasoning was that Canada needed to protect

Ambassador Julius L. Katz, President of Hills & Company, was
Chief Negotiator for NAFTA, USA.

the preferential position it had gained in its bilateral agreement with the U.S. This position was supported by the writings of a respected Canadian economist, Ron Wonnacott, who argued that a series of bilateral free trade agreements by the United States would represent a kind of "hub-and-spoke" system. The United States, as the hub would benefit more than the spokes, Canada and Mexico, each of which would be in a somewhat inferior position than if they were the single bilateral partner of the U.S.

Against this view were those who argued that Canada's trade interests in Mexico were slight and not worth the risk of another divisive political debate over free trade. In the end, those in the cabinet who favored Canada joining the negotiations between Mexico and the U.S. won the day, and Prime Minister Mulroney formally proposed to President Bush that Canada join the negotiations.

In the U.S. Government, there was also some disagreement over the inclusion of Canada in the negotiations. Concerns were expressed about the complexity that would result from a three-party negotiation, rather than one with only two parties. Strengthening this concern were the fears expressed by Mexico that Canada's inclusion would result in a more time-consuming negotiation, making it impossible to secure ratification prior to the 1992 U.S. elections, an important goal of President Salinas.

Another factor behind the support for the bilateral approach in the U.S. Government was that those advocating that approach reflected a more philosophical and more political free trade approach rather than one grounded in trade policy. Thus, concerns about the impact of bilateralism on our global trade interests were not of primary interest, nor were the details of the negotiations. Free trade was viewed as desirable in itself, and the objective from this point of view was to conclude free trade agreements where we could as fast as we could. The vision of a free trade area from Tierra del Fuego to Anchorage—set forth in President Bush's Enterprise for the Americas speech in 1990—was just that, a vision, not concerned with what the structure of the trading system might look like at the end of the day.

Interestingly, the other side of the "hub-and-spoke" argument used in Canada, that the U.S. would derive greater benefits from bilateral agreements, was not a factor in the debate in the U.S. I myself did not put a great deal of stock in the "hub-and-spoke" theory. I thought that the advantages of a core agreement, expandable to other countries far outweighed the relatively minor and transitory preferential benefits of a bilateral approach.

More important, to those of us who favored Canadian participation in the negotiations, were the serious problems we saw with a trading system moving increasingly in the direction of bilateral preferential arrangements. Were the U.S. to embark on policy of bilateral agreements, we would encourage others to do the same. What would result would be a greatly complicated trading system, with different schedules for phase-out of customs duties, different rules of origin, and different standards for investment and intellectual property. The benefits of free trade would be undermined by the increased complexity of the new structure of trade relationships.

In the end, this view carried some weight, although the awkwardness of rebuffing the Canadians was undoubtedly the decisive factor. After a series of consultations between U.S., Mexican, and Canadian trade ministers and officials, many of the Mexican concerns about timing were allayed. Canada agreed that if a tripartite agreement could not be concluded, it would gracefully step aside and not seek to impede an agreement between the U.S. and Mexico. With that, objections within the U.S. Administration to a three-way negotiation evaporated, and the NAFTA was born.

Early in the negotiations. I proposed a so-called accession clause, which would express the willingness of the NAFTA partners to entertain the participation of other countries. My reasoning was that we should, as a matter of policy, state clearly and affirmatively that the NAFTA was an open and expandable agreement.

At the same time, I did not believe that it would be possible at that time to attempt to anticipate the terms and conditions for accession, nor would it be worthwhile to attempt to negotiate them. To have attempted this would have involved further negotiations, both within the U.S. Government and with our NAFTA partners. It would have also required consultations with the Congress on something that was speculative and not very immediate.

For these reasons, the language I proposed for the NAFTA was, "This agreement is open to accession to other countries on terms and conditions to be negotiated, subject to appropriate legislative approval." There was no objection on the part of either Canada or Mexico to this idea, and the substance of my language, suitably embellished by the lawyers, was incorporated in the final text.

The only other related matter that was discussed among the negotiators was whether the accession clause should be limited to countries of the Western Hemisphere or should be silent on this point, leaving open the possibility of accession from anywhere in the world. After the briefest of discussion, it was agreed that a geographic limitation would be undesirable and that accession should be open to any country acceptable to the existing NAFTA partners.

In recent conversations I have had, and conferences I have attended, I have encountered some puzzlement and lack of understanding about the accession clause. What is the procedure, I have been asked? What are the terms and conditions? How are negotiations to be initiated?

There should be no great mystery about either the process or the conditions for entry. The process can be initiated either by a country, or by a group of countries seeking accession, or by any of the existing NAFTA partners.

The conditions of entry should, in my view, be based on whether the acceding party or parties are ready, willing and able to undertake the obligations of the NAFTA. The obligations are clearly set out in the text, but the question is whether potential candidates are pursuing the requisite non-inflationary macroeconomic policies and have the kind of political stability that would enable them to carry out the obligations of free trade in goods and services, and rules on investment and intellectual property. The decision to seek accession should, in my view, be for the acceding party or parties in the first instance. In other words, the accession should be a matter of self-selection.

What would be left to negotiate would be the transitional provisions, the time period for phase-out of the tariffs of the acceding party, and requisite changes in the institutional provisions. Such provisions, which include the Commission and dispute settlement arrangements, now based on three parties, would need to be adapted to provide for additional members.

Accession negotiations could also provide an opportunity to improve the NAFTA. It is conceivable that certain exceptions now in the text in such areas as agriculture, energy, services, transportation, and government procurement could be removed or ameliorated. Also, rules of origin could be simplified or replaced by common external tariffs on a sectoral basis, as NAFTA did with respect to television and computers.

A further question concerns how to deal with the so-called side agreements, negotiated by the Clinton Administration after the NAFTA agreement was concluded. This is likely to be a contentious area domestically and internationally, but I believe there is a middle course between the two extreme positions.

Although the basic notion of accession is fairly straightforward, in reality the process is not quite so simple. For one thing, there is the matter of negotiating with the United States of America, never a simple matter. Because of our separation of powers, the U.S. Administration cannot agree to extend the benefits of NAFTA without legislative authority.

Over the past 20 years, trade negotiations have been conducted by the President under a so-called fast-track negotiating authority, which is not so much fast as it is certain. This authority assures that if there is due notice to the Congress, agreement on the objectives of the negotiation, and adequate consultations with the Congress through the course of the negotiations, then there is a reasonable assurance that the results of the negotiation will be approved by the Congress. And importantly, what is certain is that the Congress will vote on the agreement without change. Thus, negotiating partners are assured that they will not have to conduct a second negotiation with the Congress, after having negotiated with the Administration.

Except for a very brief period in the 1980s, the President has had fast-track authority continuously since the 1974 Trade Act. That authority expired earlier this year. An effort to extend the authority as part of the Uruguay Round legislation ran into serious objections, and the Administration was forced to withdraw it so as not to jeopardize the Uruguay Round bill. While the Administration has promised to resubmit its proposal next year, its fate is uncertain.

The reasons for the failure are several. For one thing, support for fast track in the Congress has diminished. Some members resent the primary jurisdiction of the Committees on Ways and Means and Finance and the tight time constraints on floor consideration. Another complication is the impact of pay-as-you-go budget rules on trade negotiations and the unhappiness of some key members of the Congress with inclusion of the budget issues under fast track.

The primary obstacle to renewal of fast track, however, is the insistence of the Administration on adding to the authority a linkage between trade and labor and environmental objectives. Unfortunately, the Administration, in seeking an extension of fast track, succeeded only in polarizing the issue. In doing so, they failed to gain the support of labor or environmentalists. More importantly, they encountered strong objection on the part of the private sector and Congressional Republicans to the use of trade sanctions to enforce foreign labor and environmental standards. Experience with the linkage between trade and other policy interests such as human rights has persuaded the business community that the results do serious damage to our trade interests, without necessarily advancing the other policy interests.

At present there is an impasse on the matter. Even as late as last week, the Administration, in negotiating the Declaration for the Summit of the Americas, was continuing to insist on the trade linkage over the strong objections of other countries of the Hemisphere. Latest reports, however, indicate that the issue has now been finessed in the Declaration by referring to previous documents that deal with trade and the environment, without the trade linkage. This still leaves open the question of how the issue will be dealt with in respect to fast track and in subsequent negotiations.

What, then, is likely to happen on NAFTA accession? The one thing that is clear is that there will be a free trade negotiation with Chile. This was promised by President Bush as well as by President Clinton. It is now expected that at the outset of the Western Hemisphere Summit in Miami on December 9, President Clinton will announce the initiation of negotiations with Chile. While Canadian and Mexican Trade Ministers have previously stated their desire that Chile become a member of NAFTA, the U.S. has yet to state publicly whether the negotiations with Chile will be bilateral, or for accession to NAFTA. My expectation is that the President's choice will be NAFTA.

Apparently, the Administration is prepared to initiate negotiations with Chile in advance of fast track authority. In ordinary circumstances, this might be deemed a risky approach. Chile, however, is not likely to be a seriously controversial case, and with proper advance Congressional consultations, the risks of Congressional rejection of the results of a negotiation can be minimized.

Beyond Chile, the path is less clear. The Summit meeting offers a great opportunity to advance the goal of hemispheric free trade. The move toward free trade in the hemisphere is proceeding much faster than anyone would have dared to predict four years ago when President Bush set forth what he referred to as a long-term vision of hemispheric free trade. Every country of the hemisphere has now entered into one kind or another of free trade arrangement with one or more countries of the region. The arrangements, for the most part, do not parallel the NAFTA either in scope or in levels of discipline. But they do reflect a strong tide running in the direction of removal of trade barriers.

With the progress shown in the past several years in the region in terms of trade liberalization, privatization, deregulation, and macroeconomic policies directed toward the attainment of non-inflationary economic growth, the goal of a Western Hemisphere Free Trade Area, negotiated by the turn of the century, no longer seems so ambitious. The Miami Summit provides the opportunity and setting for the leaders of the hemisphere to establish that goal, and it has been reported that they will do so, with a target date of 2005 for the reaching of agreement. A work plan to achieve the goal will also be adopted by the Summit leaders, with meetings of trade ministers scheduled for June of next year and the first quarter of 1996 to assure progress toward the goal.

Nothing in the Declaration will deal directly with NAFTA accession. Reportedly, the Declaration will call for the hemispheric free trade agreement to contain the scope of the NAFTA, including investment, intellectual property, government procurement, dispute settlement, etc., with high levels of discipline.

The omission of reference to NAFTA can be understood, given the existence of other regional groupings in the hemisphere, most notably Mercosur. But speaking as a former negotiator of the NAFTA, I think it is unfortunate that the Administration has been so timid and defensive about NAFTA that it has left a void. This has left some countries, which would have preferred NAFTA accession, with no alternative but to align themselves with other groupings. This in turn has now led to the positioning of Mercosur as the core of a SAFTA, a South America Free Trade Area. It would be unfortunate if the SAFTA were to become a competitive arrangement and thus complicate attainment of the region-wide goal of hemispheric free trade.

It is interesting to note that President Clinton's greatest successes in his two years in office have been gaining the approval of NAFTA and the Uruguay Round. Hopefully the Administration will seek to build on this momentum and not shy away from pursuing an aggressive approach to the expansion of NAFTA, even as it pursues the other elements of the Summit work program. Chile provides the first opportunity to expand NAFTA, and other opportunities should be grasped as quickly as they occur.

The conclusion of the NAFTA agreement has had a major catalytic effect on the trade and economic policies of the countries of this Western Hemisphere and in Asia. The U.S. has the opportunity to continue to shape the outcome of the trend toward integration in ways that will serve both U.S. and larger world interests. But unless the U.S. continues to play the leadership role it has for the past half century, it could find events passing it by. Momentum is building toward the integration of the hemisphere. It will not wait on the U.S. The question then is what shape this integration will take. Will it take the form of a series of preferential trade agreements, with numerous exceptions, or will there be a comprehensive free trade agreement, which expands to eventually encompass all of the countries of the region?

The advantage of the NAFTA is that it is a model comprehensive agreement which should set the standard. This will depend, however, on the readiness of the U.S. to accept the accession of new members as they are ready to assume the obligations of NAFTA.

The NAFTA Treaty and the Question of Expansion: Views of the Negotiators (II)

JOHN WEEKES

Broadening or Deepening the NAFTA: NAFTA as a Liberalization or Integration Agreement?

Introduction

There is no question that there is a strong trend in favor of liberalization and regional agreements – as we shall see at the Miami Summit this weekend. At the same time, I am not confident that there is broad consensus on the issues at stake. Let me take this opportunity, therefore, to reflect on the issues involved, the pros and cons of expanding the NAFTA into an AFTA, and consider some of the institutional and policy issues that will need to be addressed.

More specifically, I would like to focus on whether NAFTA enlargement should involve *broadening a trade liberalization agreement* or *deepening an economic integration agreement*. Is the NAFTA to be the basis for a regional integration agreement similar in scope and content to the EU or will it continue as a GATT—or

John Weekes is Senior Assistant Deputy Minister and Coordinator for the NAFTA, Ministry of Foreign Affairs and International Trade, Canada.

WTO—plus regional liberalization agreement? The difference is important and the implications are significant.

2. A Single Trade Policy

To start, I think it is important that we understand the difference between ends and means. The past decade has seen an intense level of trade negotiation involving a multiplicity of instruments. All of these instruments—from the Canada-U.S. FTA, through the NAFTA to the new WTO—are all means that should lead us to a common objective: the development of more open, rules-based economic exchanges on a global basis.

The proliferation of trade agreements and the development of a tripolar economic world may give the impression that there is conflict between global and regional rule making. There are times when that may be the case, but looked at from a sufficiently long-term perspective, I have no hesitation in stating that Canada is pursuing a single objective, but is more prepared than in the past to use a wider range of means to achieve that objective.

3. Lessons from the Past: the Triumph of Policy

Against that background, does NAFTA expansion make trade policy sense? Would expanding the NAFTA to Chile and others solve problems, extend benefits, create opportunities that cannot be addressed on the basis of existing rules/agreements/institutions, or through much simpler and less complicating arrangements?

Governments do not/should not invest scarce political and negotiating coinage in such agreements for short-term political advantages, to create "announcables."

Why should governments want to negotiate fixed-rule, liberalizing trade agreements? Four fundamental reasons suggest themselves:

- economic reasons—comparative advantage, specialization, and the international division of labor based on trade all point toward increases in global economic welfare. While there may be individual/concentrated losses from more open global trade and investment conditions, in aggregate the gains far outweigh the losses. For economists that thesis is captured by the word "free."

- **commercial reasons**—such agreements expand trade and investment opportunities for internationally competitive firms within a stable and predictable framework of rules. Without such agreements, international trade and investment would be no more than a gambler's throw. For business, the word is "opportunity."

- **legal reasons**—rules/clarity/principles/due process in conflict resolution—all point to a more orderly, predictable and fairer world. For lawyers the word is "fair."

- **political reasons**—an orderly and principled manner in which to achieve the first three goals—such agreements allow governments to pursue gains while providing room to manage adjustment from losses. For politicians the word is "equitable."

The record of the past 60 years—from Cordell Hull's RTA program to the WTO—is a record of achievement and success in meeting these goals. There may have been setbacks and disappointments along the way, but there is no question that we can look back and see the steady establishment of a policy that has worked.

The past ten years—the FTA/NAFTA/WTO—has been a period of highly charged debate and very active negotiating agenda, and also a period of extraordinary progress and success. The success of the past, however, underpins the need to go further now. In effect, the success of more than five decades of trade liberalization, underwritten by various international trade agreements, now points to the need to move to more comprehensive or integrative agreements.

From that perspective, we need to consider whether NAFTA is an appropriate means and to what extent the various players are interested in using it as either a trade liberalization or an economic integration agreement. As it stands, NAFTA contains elements of both and can be used as a vehicle to achieve either set of goals. The direction chosen, however, has important implications for the design of the agreement and the goals to be pursued.

The decision to proceed in one direction or the other, however, should involve an assessment of two sets of important contextual factors: the changing nature of international business and the recent record of success in negotiating more far-reaching trade agreements.

4. The New, Global Information Economy

The changing nature of the organization of production—global and information-based—means that increasingly, markets are no longer national, but local, regional and global, and that it has become more and more difficult to differentiate what is domestic from what is foreign. In response, we are seeing the beginning of a new trade policy that moves well beyond the simple goal of trade liberalization and closer to the more complex and politically difficult goal of economic integration.

The Europeans have moved further along the path of experimenting with the demands of this new trade policy. The EU—in its rules and institutions—is a much more integrative agreement than either the NAFTA or the WTO. In effect, the EU has developed a scheme of regulation which has allowed a group of 12—soon 15—countries to maintain their separate identities and political priorities while creating a single market now as integrated as that of the 50 states. There are *no* customs procedures, no antidumping provisions, no buy-national procurement preferences, no market limiting product standards. There *are* EU-wide rules about competition, subsidies, and restrictive business practices. And there is a Commission, Parliament and Court to enforce these provisions.

In the NAFTA, on the other hand, there *are* customs procedures, antidumping provisions, buy-national procurement preferences, and market limiting product standards. There are *no* NAFTA-wide rules about competition, subsidies or restrictive business practices. And there is no independent Commission, Parliament or Court to enforce NAFTA's provisions. In short, the NAFTA is a WTO-plus regional *liberalization* agreement rather than an EU-like regional *integration* agreement.

This is not an accident. In the original Canada-U.S. FTA and then in the NAFTA negotiations, the parties to the agreement did not set out to negotiate a regional integration agreement. They set out to liberalize trade among themselves and at the same time address some of the newer issues which would, of necessity, move them closer to an integration agreement. The U.S. sought to make progress on services, investment and intellectual property while Canada and Mexico wanted to pursue competition-type issues. Progress was made on these issues, but in a cautious, GATT-like manner. There is still no evidence that the three signatories of the NAFTA are agreed on moving beyond GATT-like commitments to EU-type rules.

In the United States, and to some extent in Canada, there has been much preoccupation with sovereignty, based on a conviction that the more integrative an agreement becomes, the more sovereignty its members cede to non-accountable rules and institutions. In my view, that is a profound misreading of reality. The kinds of integrative agreements I have in mind do not involve a loss of sovereignty but a way for democratic societies to reassert control over economic transactions in a global economy. In effect, collective rule-making recaptures political authority lost as a result of the silent integration flowing from globalization. That is how I read the spate of new agreements negotiated over the past decade.

5. The WTO—a New Beginning

Over the past ten years, we have seen regional and global negotiations aimed at addressing the transition from trade among a set of interlinked national economies to trade and investment within an integrated global economy, ranging from the deeply integrative EC-92/Single European Act, to the mixed FTA/NAFTA, and the liberalizing World Trade Organization (WTO). The success of these efforts should both condition and influence the next steps, including the question of broadening and/or deepening the NAFTA.

We have to decide whether we want to take the NAFTA as the basis for more intensive regional liberalization or as a basis for a more far-reaching regional integration agreement. That is not just an issue for the potential new applicants. It is also an issue for the original signatories.

What may have made sense for Canada and the United States 10 years ago, or for Canada, the United States and Mexico five years ago, does not necessarily make sense for the Americas today. The global trade policy context in which the issue of first the Canada-U.S. FTA and then the NAFTA were considered is significantly different from the global trade policy context in which an AFTA is being considered.

Ten years ago, i.e., 1984-85, when Canada and the United States thought about a bilateral FTA, they did so against the background of a failed GATT ministerial, a frustration at the inability of the multilateral forum to address issues of critical importance to the bilateral relationship.

Five years ago, i.e., in 1989-90, when Mexico contemplated an FTA and the U.S. and Canada responded, they did so against the background of a less than-satisfactory mid-term review of the Uruguay Round in 1988 and a failure to bring the round to a successful conclusion in 1990.

Today, consideration of an AFTA needs to take place against a very different background: 10 years of extremely productive trade policy making and trade negotiations culminating in the successful conclusion of the Uruguay Round and the probable establishment of a WTO and its important new range of multilateral agreements on January 1, 1995.

Indeed, in making a frank assessment of the NAFTA and the WTO, the number of areas where the NAFTA is more liberalizing and/or more integrating, i.e., provides a superior set of rules and conditions, is not nearly as significant as some might think. Let me suggest where the most significant differences lie:

- once fully implemented, access for goods is tariff free – but, that is offset by the transaction costs created by strict rules of origin, particularly for developing countries who already benefit from GSP and CBI treatment;

- customs rules are better and customs-based conflicts are more easily resolved;

- the investment chapter provides the best rules available, including investor-state arbitration;

- the chapter XIX binational panel provisions for anti-dumping and countervailing duty cases are a real plus, but should be seen as no more than a temporary solution—the real issue is the continued availability of rules that should have no place in an integration agreement; and

- some sectoral rules are better, e.g., autos, agriculture and textiles and clothing.

Offsetting these advantages is the fact that the WTO is a multilateral, global set of rules with a strong, independent secretariat capable of helping smaller members and with general dispute settlement provisions that are now more than the equal of NAFTA chapter XX, particularly in view of the independent legal advice provided to panels by the WTO's legal division.

Nevertheless, we have to recognize that the NAFTA has proved both symptomatic and catalytic of a new attitude. It has stimulated imagination not only in the Western Hemisphere, but also across the Pacific, adding to the momentum of trade liberalization and the global trade reform movement. In short, it has produced a bandwagon effect. Its impact has been as much psychological as real.

This bandwagon effect has many positive dimensions. At the same time, we should not let it stampede us into policy directions that may complicate the important goals we are trying to achieve—a better functioning global economy, global welfare and individual prosperity.

6. Mixed Motives

Against that background, the issue of NAFTA deepening or broadening is not just a matter of signing up a number of countries in Central and South America. Expanding the NAFTA has implications for the three existing signatories, for the functioning of the global trading system as a whole, for the economic development of the countries of Latin America, and for the prospect of deepening or enlarging its integrative elements. From that perspective, the motives and interests of the various players are not all complementary and mutually reinforcing.

Virtually all the potential players—Canada, the U.S., Mexico, most Latin American countries, and even some Asia-Pacific countries—can agree on a basic set of motives and objectives that could be served by expanding the NAFTA, including:

- improving and expanding access to the markets of the region, leading to new trade and investment opportunities;
- maintaining the positive momentum of the FTA/NAFTA/WTO;

- extending and even expanding a positive trade policy for the Third World—NAFTA and the WTO are a major improvement over GATT's earlier miserable record. An AFTA would also be infinitely better than the proliferation of overlapping and contradictory bilateral and/or sub-regional agreements; and

- locking in the significant political and economic reforms already undertaken by countries throughout Latin America, while providing tangible support to Latin America's continuing efforts at democratization.

These are all motives that fit in well with using the NAFTA as an expanding vehicle to promote broader trade liberalization. Using the NAFTA as a vehicle for deepening integration, either within North America or more broadly, brings forward a different set of issues, such as:

- Government procurement—moving from GATT-like commitments based on specific entities to national treatment;

- Trade remedies—moving from GATT-like procedural safeguards to common rules about competition and subsidies;

- Services—moving from commitments about negative lists to common standards and mutual recognition;

- Investment—moving further down the track to domestic enforcement of common rules and procedures;

- Institutional—moving from ad hoc intra-regional to supranational arrangements involving commission and court-like structures; and

- Sovereignty—addressing some very major implications.

If we are going to proceed, now is the time to think such matters through, set realistic goals and establish a process that will lead to positive results rather than a muddle of good intentions and half-baked agreements. In short, we need to determine whether we want to use the NAFTA as a basis for expanding and consolidating trade liberalization or whether we want to use it as a vehicle for moving further along the path of economic integration. Do we see the NAFTA as a WTO-plus agreement, or as the basis for an EU-type of agreement for the Americas?

7. Problems and Issues

Is it possible to broaden and deepen at the same time? Does expansion now mean dilution? There are arguments on both sides of the question. NAFTA suggests you can deepen/strengthen an existing agreement while expanding it to a new partner. Other experiences point in the other direction.

Few countries are as ready today as Mexico was five years ago and none have the special factors of geographic proximity and degree of integration and trade dependence that made the Mexican case compelling. At the same time, Latin American readiness needs to be determined by them; the role of Canada and the United States should be to determine whether we want to provide the opportunity.

For Canada, for example, expansion may divert attention and energy away from important issues in the Canada-U.S. trade and economic relationship. While this consideration may be of minor significance in Washington, it is of major consequence in Ottawa. In the view of some, the emerging issues are ones that are more likely to be addressed in a Canada-U.S. context than a hemispheric one.

Concentrating on expanding the NAFTA into a WTO-plus AFTA may also risk dilution of global rule making. While there are solid reasons to accept that there is a place for both global and re-gional rule-making in the more complex, multi-tier world that emerged in the 1980s, the factors that make a Canada-U.S. or a NAFTA agreement natural (e.g., proximity, degree of integration, extent of bilateral trade and investment, etc.), such factors are not present in the rest of the hemisphere. Successful implementation of the WTO provides the countries of the region with both a challenging and a viable set of rules for the immediate future.

Finally, expanding the NAFTA into an AFTA may alienate our trading partners across the Atlantic and Pacific who might well question the motives involved. Would an AFTA be a building block or a stumbling block to a better functioning global regime? There are arguments in both directions.

8. Conclusions — the Bottom Line

On balance, some useful goals can be achieved through NAFTA expansion to the rest of the hemisphere. Generally, these are important goals but devoting negotiating coin and energy to them may have a negative impact on the pursuit of other important goals. These negative aspects, however, can be managed if dealt with carefully. The United States, more for political than economic reasons, appears to be interested in expanding the NAFTA, which means Canada will want to be involved.

Over the next 10 years, interest in Latin America is likely to lead to an enlargement of the NAFTA. As we proceed down that path, however, it is important that we take stock and determine what kind of NAFTA we want—do we want one that provides a basis for further integration along hemispheric lines or one that promotes liberalization and as much integration as is absolutely necessary, but no more? In short, do we want to use the NAFTA to leap or crawl into the future? In either event let's do it with our eyes open.

Economic Benefits of NAFTA and Hemispheric Integration (I)

ALAN REYNOLDS

The Benefits of NAFTA in Retrospect

It is often tempting to define the benefits of freer trade in terms of what it will do for producers. If other countries (such as Mexico) lower their tariffs, we can export more. We may have to lower our own tariffs in exchange, which is a pity, but the expanded export markets make this sacrifice worthwhile.

There is a name for the idea that countries should try to maximize exports and minimize imports. This curious notion—that a country benefits from what it sells and loses from what it buys—is called "mercantilism." Adam Smith set out to debunk the mercantilists in 1776. He easily won the argument, but you'd never know that by listening to the recent controversy over NAFTA and GATT.

If he were still around, Smith would emphasize that the main beneficiary of lower trade barriers in North America is *consumers*, not producers. We produce only in order to consume. Since lower tariffs let us consume more and better products at lower prices, our living standards improve. Lower tariffs and quotas mean more variety, more competition, and lower prices. For industries that used to be protected in all three NAFTA countries, this is very bad news. Freer

Alan Reynolds is senior fellow and Director of Economic Research at Hudson Institute.

trade and tougher competition make it much harder to gouge consumers with high prices, indifferent service and shoddy products. Competition is wonderful for consumers, but difficult and dangerous for producers.

Ross Perot's odd book on NAFTA devoted a few pages to fretting about the U.S. broom industry. Amazingly, the broom industry really was a significant anti-NAFTA force in several Congressional districts, just as protected sugar, tobacco, peanut and citrus industries managed to sway votes against NAFTA in the affected districts.

Perot failed to mention that brooms have been protected by a 32 percent tariff. Why should U.S. consumers pay 32 percent extra for brooms? To save jobs? But people buy *fewer* brooms at the higher price, not more; and they substitute plastic brooms, vacuum cleaners and leaf blowers. In any case, tying straw on a stick is not exactly on the cutting edge of high technology, not the sort of job we send our kids to college for. Let Mexico make the brooms, and thereby earn the dollars to buy from the U.S. the lumber, corn straw, paint and lathes they'll need to make more brooms. Let them make the children's T-shirts, and thus earn the dollars they'll need to buy U.S. cotton and fabric. "Save Our Sweatshops" is not an appropriate motto for the United States in the 21st Century.

For most U.S. industries, which had little or no trade protection before NAFTA, the trade agreement is a marvelous blessing. They gain greater access to the young and rapidly growing Mexican market. But the main point remains that reducing U.S. tariffs was good for the U.S., even if Mexico and Canada had not reciprocated. Lower U.S. tariffs reduce our cost of living and cost of production, making us richer. Lower Mexican and Canadian tariffs have the same effect in Mexico and Canada. There may be some adjustment problems, moving labor and capital out of previously protected industries, but the welfare gain to the whole nation is sizable and unambiguous.

Let's apply Smithian economics to modern mercantilists who continue to oppose NAFTA, or its extension to other Latin American countries.

The Joint Economic Committee "Study"

On December 1, Senator Byron Dorgan of North Dakota released a so-called Joint Economic Committee "study"—reportedly produced by Rob Scott, who was prudent to leave his name off of it. This six-page "study" says that if a billion dollars of exports create 20,000 jobs, then a billion of imports must destroy 20,000 jobs (though that doesn't really follow). Since U.S. imports of goods from Mexico increased by 23 percent from January to September, while U.S. exports to Mexico increased by "only" 22 percent, the JEC figures that the imports destroyed 137,000 jobs, while the exports added 127,000 jobs—for a *net* loss of 10,000 jobs.

Note that this is a much stronger claim than that made by those who cite the fact that a similar number are claiming benefits under NAFTA's adjustment assistance program. That program is quite generous, even to those who claim a vague "indirect" injury, and class-action lawyers are ingenious about finding ways to get federal money. But even if 10,000 workers really were displaced from previously protected U.S. industries, the *net* job gain in the U.S. would still be well over 100,000 in nine months, by the JEC's arithmetic.

The U.S. is still running a large trade *surplus* with Mexico in 1994—despite big U.S. imports of Mexican crude oil and vegetables. The U.S. surplus in manufactured goods is huge, and net agricultural exports through September were up 1,040 percent, to over a quarter of a billion dollars. Yet the fact that the trade surplus shrunk a bit compared with last year is nonetheless described by the JEC as losing U.S. jobs, as though Mexico could and should run big trade deficits forever. Moreover, the JEC study completely ignores *services*, which was a major objective of NAFTA negotiators from the U.S. The U.S. exported $10 billion in services to Mexico in 1992, even though many service exports were tightly restricted at that time—before NAFTA.

U.S. merchandise imports from *all* countries have been soaring, because the U.S. economy has been growing much faster than the economies of Japan or Europe, until very recently, and much faster than the economy of Mexico as well. The U.S. merchandise trade deficit increased by 28 percent in the first three quarters. The U.S. is importing a lot because demand is strong and we are close to capacity in several key industries, such as autos and machinery. U.S. imports *always* grow rapidly when GDP does, and imports likewise contract only in recessions. According to the JEC's mercantilist math, *recessions must increase employment by reducing imports*!

The JEC tables reveal that over 65 percent of the shrinkage in the U.S. trade surplus with Mexico was due to increased U.S. imports of crude oil. A growing U.S. economy needs more oil, and we might as well buy it from our neighbor. Actually, the fact that U.S. exports to Mexico have risen almost as fast as imports was quite unusual, because the Mexican economy was virtually stagnant in 1993 and early 1994, only rebounding a bit in the second and third quarters.

The JEC paper says "the U.S. is exporting raw materials and parts to Mexico, and importing final products of greater value." Of greater value? The study's own figures show a merchandise trade *surplus* with Mexico of $1.75 billion in the first three quarters, compared with $1.8 billion in the same period last year. What is meant, apparently, is that Mexico "adds value" when it puts a U.S. picture tube in a television set, or U.S. upholstery in a car. Of course they do. Value-added is just another name for GDP. Nobody is going to produce anything if they can't add some value.

Well, we don't pay economists at the JEC very well, and politicians get what they pay for—cheap propaganda.

Pat Buchanan recently wrote another hysterical column that ended, "guess where your next Ford Escort is coming from?" If you know anything about small cars, your next one will be a Chrysler Neon from Michigan or a Saturn from Tennessee. But even if you end up stuck with an Escort, and it happens to be the station wagon version which, is indeed assembled in Mexico, it is going to be officially classified as a U.S. car. Why? Because it has an 80 percent U.S. content.

The JEC paper shows that U.S. exports of nonelectrical machinery to Mexico are up 68 percent so far this year, while exports of transportation equipment (cars and trucks) are up 85 percent, chemicals 37 percent, paper 33 percent, and textile exports up 21 percent. The JEC insinuates that soaring U.S. exports of "raw materials and parts"—which means machinery, chemicals, fabric and paper—are inherently inferior to Mexico's exports of "finished goods." But that is simply wrong if most of the value-added is in the U.S.—as in the case with the Ford Escort. After all, a broom or T-shirt is a "finished good," while a massive piece of industrial or farm equipment, or a ton of sophisticated chemicals, is not.

When it comes to the benefits of expanding NAFTA, the mercantilist arguments of World Bank economists are similar to those at the JEC. Two World Bank economists recently wrote a paper entitled "Free Trade Agreements with the United States: What's In It for Latin America?" The argument, believe it or not, was that since U.S. trade barriers are already quite low, because of the Generalized System of Preferences, there is little point in Latin American countries enduring the sacrifice of reducing their own tariffs and import quotas: "The average level of tariff protection in most Latin American countries is considerably higher than in the United States, and the potential for an FTA-induced expansion of U.S. exports appears considerably greater than for Latin America in the North American market." Latin American exports might only rise "by roughly 8 or 9 percent," the World Bank economists argued, so why should Latin America bother cutting tariffs? If they really do not know the answer to that question, they really do not know anything at all about economics.

If we pursue such mercantilist arguments to their illogical conclusion, it follows that the best possible policy a country could follow would be to export *everything* it produces and accept *nothing* in exchange—no goods, at least, only IOUs. This would supposedly maximize employment, according to JEC reasoning, though it would also have the unfortunate side effect of leaving the people in a protectionist paradise with no cars, no clothes and no food. It wouldn't work anyway, since other countries could not long afford to buy such a country's products if they could not earn that country's currency by exporting goods and services.

If exporting without importing was really the best way to increase employment, as the JEC and World Bank economists seem to believe, the same effect could be achieved quite easily. Simply load up some U.S. ships with U.S. cars and planes, and then sink the ships at sea with a U.S. bomb. Look at all the jobs we'd create building the next ship, and loading it up again!

The benefits from trade are from what we *import*, not what we export. Exports are the price we have to pay, sooner or later, for the imports. But getting a bargain on imports is always better than paying more—paying that tax we call a tariff. Cutting inexcusable taxes on trade in a few politically-favored industries is what NAFTA is all about. All the diversionary tactics we saw repeated in the GATT debate—such as pretending that civilized dispute settlement procedures mean a loss of sovereignty—were simply special-interest propaganda designed to conceal this simple truth.

The anti-NAFTA campaign was always bad economics and worse politics. Most candidates who ran against NAFTA followed Ross Perot and Pat Buchanan into political oblivion—including James Jontz and Joe Hogsett here in Indiana, and Perot adviser Richard Fisher in Texas.

The French economist Frederic Bastiat explained the benefits of NAFTA over a century ago. We are all producers and consumers, but in our capacity as consumers we prefer abundance and low prices. In our capacity as producers, on the other hand, we are apt to lobby for artificial scarcity and high prices. A country in which politics typically caters to producers ends up, of course, with scarcity and high prices.

NAFTA and GATT were unusually impressive victories of consumers over the awesome political clout of special interests. Adding more nations to NAFTA will mean more affluent consumers in more nations.

Economic Benefits of NAFTA and Hemispheric Integration (II)

RIORDAN ROETT

Four quick points on politics—I leave the economic issues to the economists. The topic that I want to address first is the political dynamic of regional integration. Second, the issue of capital flows and investment, which at bottom is political. You make decisions based on perceptions of political stability, as well as economic opportunity. Third, the Miami Summit. Is anything going to happen? Should anything happen? And finally, the importance of hemispheric integration to the social agenda in the Americas and ultimately to political stability, which should be our ultimate concern.

More important than the impressive gains in trade due to NAFTA, I think, is the Summit that is taking place this weekend, which may mark a definitive turning point in terms of the southern cone's future. I am not talking about Miami; I am talking about Essen, Germany where the European Union will hold a summit on December 9 and 10. My good friend Wolf Grabendorff, who I saw two weeks ago in Madrid and who is the director of the Institute for European-Latin America Relations of the European Union, based in Madrid, told me that this hemisphere will be a high priority. The

Dr. Riordan Roett is Senior Political Analyst in the International Capital Markets group of Chase Manhattan Bank. He is on leave from the Johns Hopkins School of Advanced International Studies, where he is Sarita and Don Johnson Professor of International Relations.

message is that Europe, having maintained strong economic relations with South America during the debt distress decade of the 1980s, does not plan to abandon the region to the U.S. now that it is enjoying some economic success. If approved by the Summit in Essen—which may be, from the South Americans' point of view, as relevant as what is not going to happen in Miami with our Summit—there will be a new package announced by the European Union that will include plans to enhance economic relations with Mexico; to extend the Generalized System of Preferences arrangements with the Andean countries and Central America; and most importantly to approve the decision to move forward with the negotiations on a common market with Mercosur.

What's important to point out as well is that the European Union, since 1986, has become the largest trading partner with the four members of the Mercosur. The southern cone is by far the fastest growing market for European exports. In 1992, the European Union accounted for 27 percent of Mercosur exports against 21 percent for North America, 48 percent of direct foreign investment, and Mercosur received 42 percent of European Union foreign aid. The proposal of the Commission at Essen, which is more important perhaps to the southern cone than the Miami Summit, given the lack of leadership so far in Miami by this administration, is to gradually establish a free trade zone in industrial goods and reciprocal and progressive liberalization of farm trade—as always in Europe, this is the kicker, taking in to account the sensitivity of certain farm products.

The political point, though, is that the Europeans are coming back into the southern cone in a big way. One of our problems in the United States is of course that we are so focused on Mexico and Central America for historic and geopolitical reasons that we seldom seem to get below Venezuela, save when there is a crisis. The dynamics of what may be happening—I am not saying it will happen, but may be happening—between the European Union and Mercosur, the growth of Mercosur and the reason Mercosur hasn't functioned is quite obvious, isn't it? It's been the incompetence of the Brazilian government. But that incompetence is now about to disappear. A brand new economic team and a new political leader who has endorsed Mercosur will indeed provide, I think, the leadership required to make this a very important and vital link.

Second, another regional dynamic which is terribly important, of course, is APEC. As you know, President Clinton has made a great deal out of APEC. Chile became the 18th member of the Asian-Pacific group during the recent meeting in Indonesia. APEC indeed includes all of the current NAFTA countries. And at the meeting in Indonesia, the 18 members made a commitment to a continuing process of high level negotiation. They called for a detailed blueprint, with dates for regional liberalization, before their next Summit in Osaka in 1995.

If we get that much out of Miami, a blueprint with dates for the hemisphere, we'll be very, very lucky. And given the disarray in the White House, the resignation of Lloyd Bentsen, the inability to find a true line for determining trade policy for the entire hemisphere—not just for Mexico, or the Caribbean or Central America—I doubt we'll do that well.

There are thus two important political dynamics that somebody at some point in Washington is going to have to consider—the Mercosur, with its links to Europe and elsewhere, and APEC. How does all of this fit in to a very strong and dynamic role by the United States?

Second, it is important to look at the financial aspects of the hemisphere. As we all know, to a great degree NAFTA was not about trade, it was about investment. That's critical. Sid Weintraub and I just came back from the inauguration of Ernesto Zedillo. One of the pieces of paper we were given as we registered, was the Ministry of Trade and Industry's announcement that direct foreign investment in Mexico during November 1994 (through November 28) was $1.61 billion—the highest monthly total recorded during the administration of Carlos Salinas de Gortati. The figure represents an increase of 300 percent over the average monthly amount of direct foreign investment in the country during the six years of the Salinas Administration. The majority of the investment that has flowed into Mexico has been channeled into the nation's productive sector.

Investment is what it is all about, following trade. If we don't get on with trade, it is not a question of whether or not the investment flows are going to continue and are going to augment—which is critical of course—to cover the current account deficits in these countries and more importantly to get into the productive sector, which indeed allows them to increase the sophistication of their exports. So someone has got to make a link in Miami between trade and investment and come up with some bright answers as to what happens if we don't move forward with the kind of economic and trade integration that is required for Latin America.

Third, I think that some important political questions with regard to the Miami Summit have been raised given the recent defeat of the Democratic party in the mid-term elections, the resignation of the Secretary of the Treasury, and other events. Now the *Financial Times* had a report this morning, a rather cute report, quoting the U.S. trade negotiator, Mr. Kantor, saying that they want a symbolic gesture at the end of the evening, the last evening of the Miami Summit. That will be the announcement that they will go forward with negotiations with regard to Chile. The only problem, of course, is that the announcement also said U.S. officials see a chance for passage of fast-track authority limited to Chile. Now, if you talk to Republican members of the House and the Senate, and you ask if the votes exist at this moment for fast-track authorization, even for Chile, which is looked at with a very sympathetic eye in Washington for a whole set of political and economic reasons, the answer is negative.

There is an awful lot of homework that therefore needs to be done to indeed bring Chile in. As you know, Chile is one of the smaller economies of South America compared to the NAFTA members. It is one-sixth the size of Mexico, a twentieth of the United States, and most of its exports to the United States are already at zero or low tariffs. I'm not sure what's symbolic for Mickey Kantor and Bill Clinton on Sunday night is relevant in terms of the overall movement towards integration in the hemisphere.

My fourth point is the importance of moving forward briskly with programs to address the social problems in Latin America and to sustain political stability.

One of the things that Ernesto Zedillo said on December 1 is that he is declaring war on poverty. The Lagniappe conference in New York reported that the poorest 20 percent of the Mexican population, which held 4.8 percent of the income in 1984 in Mexico, now holds just 4.3 percent, while the richest 20 percent, which held 49.5 percent in 1984, now holds 55.8 percent. Do you know how many billionaires there are now in Mexico?

President Samper in Colombia has announced a major social investment program. Aninat and Frei in Chile have announced that in the next five years, the major objective in budget allocations will be in education, to add value to Chilean exports.

Slowly the countries are coming around to the importance of social investment. But clearly a very strong and positive lead on trade to create new jobs and to generate exports is required to maintain the level of investment required in the social sector in Latin America. In turn, that is tied directly, to the maintenance of democratic and stable political institutions.

In a sense, the bottom line, then, is what price are we willing to pay in the next century in Latin America to avoid social and political instability. To preclude instability, we need strong, rational leadership on trade and investment in the United States.

Economic Benefits of NAFTA and Hemispheric Integration (III)

ROBERTO SALINAS-LEÓN

A Mexican Perspective

Introduction

The peso devaluation in Mexico has generated widespread suspicion throughout the American hemisphere about the feasibility of market-oriented models of economic organization. A central aspect of Mexico's program of structural economic reform is the North American Free trade Agreement (NAFTA). Consequently, the entire notion of open trade in the hemispheric continent as proposed in the Miami Summit has been called into question. This is the political fallout of the 'tequila" effect, which Mexico's currency collapse has engendered in emerging financial markets. In other words, the peso devaluation has unwittingly invited NAFTA-bashers into the forefront of policy discussions about hemispheric liberalization.

The current state of affairs constitutes a dramatic test of the strategic benefits of NAFTA in forcing public policy to undertake issue-specific measures such as greater liberalization and a more

Dr. Roberto Salinas-León is Executive Director of the Centro de Investigaciones Sobre la Libre Empresa (Center for Free Enterprise Research) in Mexico City. He has testified twice before the U.S. Congress in defense of NAFTA. This paper is a revised version of Dr. Salinas's remarks at the Indianapolis Summit.

profound privatization process as mechanisms designed to restore confidence and increase the competitiveness of the Mexican economy. Indeed, a salient irony about the current politics of NAFTA is that it has gained far broader support in the Latin American region (that is, a region with long statist and protectionist traditions) than in the U.S., the supposed bastion of free trade and free markets.

As the Miami agenda materializes, the countries now exploring the possibility of becoming part of the NAFTA trade framework are likely to focus on the same questions and concerns which were addressed by Mexico—including proper exchange-rate policy. For this reason, the Mexican case represents a model of what is likely to ensue (other things being equal) in other nations which gain admission into the agreement. So construed, Mexico's role in continental trade liberalization is critical: It acts as a commercial and cultural bridge between the rich North American region and the underdeveloped Latin American region.

An Update of NAFTA

In a special trade summit held in Guadalajara in 1994, former Undersecretary of Trade, Pedro Noyola, delighted a mostly pro-NAFTA audience by stating that "sucking sounds are for suckers." The allusion to Ross Perot's cheap claim that NAFTA would created a "great sucking sound" of jobs fleeing south in search of cheap labor was obvious, but so was Noyola's conviction that trade liberalization between the U.S. and Mexico *has produced and will continue to produce more job opportunities in both countries.* This conviction now boasts solid evidential support. The first results of NAFTA show that it has had a welcome impact on Mexico's export growth, a positive effect on the flow of new foreign investment, and has enabled the nation to consolidate a more competitive position in the global marketplace.

The NAFTA treaty establishes a framework that enables 84 percent of Mexico's non-oil exports to enter the U.S. market duty and quota-free (this is equivalent to 7,300 products). Conversely, some 40 percent of U.S. and Canadian exports can enter the Mexican market under the same conditions. The vast majority of *this* percentage is composed of intermediary durables not made or sold in the domestic market and capital-intensive goods such as machinery, high-tech equipment, systems, and the like.

This global trade privilege has paid off significantly in the first six months of NAFTA's implementation. In this period, Mexico's exports to the U.S. registered an overwhelming increase of 20.5 percent, which is significantly more than the international average of 8.4 percent. In particular, manufactured export goods saw a 23.8 percent jump, whereas exports to the rest of the world witnessed an increase of 15.8 percent. The nation's top exports include automobiles, electronic goods, machinery parts, plastics, computers and glass. Imports from the U.S. have also seen a significant boost, with a 10.8 percent growth rate for the same period, and 36.8 percent from Canada. An estimated 88 percent of this figure has been capital-intensive and intermediary goods.

What do these figures mean? The increase of two-way trade between Mexico and the U.S. is expected to increase to a massive $125 billion U.S. by the end of 1994. Thus, *Mexico surpassed Japan to become the U.S.'s second most important export market.* This has supplied new job opportunities for both economies. According to the U.S. Trade Representative Office, every $1 billion in new exports is equivalent to some 19,000 new higher-paid (skilled and semi-skilled) jobs. This means that in the ten months since the implementation of NAFTA, the U.S. has been able to expand its labor market by some 200,000 new, higher-paying jobs.

In addition, an important byproduct of NAFTA is that the treaty allows for the gradual entry of U.S. and other foreign financial institutions into Mexico. The approval of 18 new banking subsidiaries and other financial services organizations represents an investment of $1.5 billion in the short term, which is equivalent to 4,000 new jobs south of the U.S. border. As a result of an emergency program of stabilization to restore confidence in Mexico's financial markets, the Zedillo government is in the process of revising foreign investment legislation governing financial services in order to enable overseas institutions to invest in the nation's domestic banking assets. Prior to 1995, foreign investment in local banks was restricted to 30 percent ownership in non-voting shares.

The implementation of NAFTA also reflects the accord's potential contribution towards fulfilling the capital needs of a severely undercapitalized economy, depleted by the inherent wastefulness of the statism and protectionism of the past. Official estimates claim that Mexico needs a 10-year total inflow of $150 billion to service the capital requirements of a rapidly expanding workforce. This is a staggering $15 billion per year. NAFTA was negotiated to meet this challenge, by consolidating a reliable investment regime. It does so by institutionalizing national treatment of foreign investors and by eliminating cumbersome performance requirements. Indeed, despite the erosion of confidence in currency markets and public policy decision-making, the Mexican economy is projected to receive an inflow of $48 billion in new investment in 1995. This is double the amount the economy received prior to the advent of NAFTA.

Since the U.S. ratification of NAFTA in November 1993, Mexico has captured *over $15 billion in new private capital investment flows*. Thus, despite marked political and financial instability, foreign investment continues to grow at a positive pace. In 1994, Mexico received over $11 billion in new foreign investment. This brings the sum total in the Salinas administration to $53.7 billion U.S.—*111 percent higher* than the original six-year projection of $25 billion set in 1989. In short, *more money has flowed into Mexico since NAFTA was first proposed in 1990 than at any other time during the 20th century.*

So construed, the key point about NAFTA to Mexico is not unrestricted market access, but that the treaty encourages *market-oriented reform* by locking in macroeconomic policies of balanced budgets, privatization and trade liberalization. This, despite the current crisis, translates into positive long-term prospects for the development of a profitable economic climate.

The political opponents of free-trade in the U.S. did themselves a disservice when they deployed ill-founded claims about mass unemployment to argue against NAFTA. So far, the early evidence corroborates the simple logical point that free-trade maximizes commerce, and more open commerce means more jobs, not less. To this extent, Noyola's assessment of the "sucking sound theory" appears to be right on the mark.

Liberalization in the Americas

The strategic impact of full continental trade in Latin America and the Caribbean is a welcome aspect of extending NAFTA beyond the North American borders. In addition, other arguments highlight the importance of an arrangement like NAFTA for the region's private sector. There are four fundamental reasons for the desirability of forging closer commercial ties under the NAFTA framework, everywhere from Chile to Curacao. In general, the treaty implies more business for inter-American business.

The first argument centers on the need for order. Latin America and the U.S. already enjoy a flourishing trade relationship. In 1992, multilateral trade exceeded $80 billion. This trade inertia will continue with or without a NAFTA-style arrangement. The NAFTA framework represents an attempt to consolidate legal order in this growing trade relationship.

The need for a neutral dispute settlement mechanism, for instance, is evident in view of the problem of "unilateralism", namely, the problem that U.S. accusations of antidumping practices or failure to meet environmental standards, as in the case of the Mexican tuna embargo, Ecuadorean coffee and Chilean fruit, were decided in U.S. courts. The cross-selection dispute solving mechanism embodied in NAFTA avoids this problem by seeking neutrality in deciding trade disputes among the three countries. This will prove highly beneficial for Latin America and the Caribbean.

The Latin American and Caribbean markets enjoy enormous potential for trade liberalization. The region has a population of 460 million consumers and GDP valued at close to $1 trillion, with total world trade of $245 billion. Such facts reveal that an agreement along NAFTA lines is superior to a myriad of bilateral arrangements.

The second argument for NAFTA centers on diversification. In effect, open trade liberalization has greatly transformed the structure of Mexico's external sector. The latter has diversified its exports and performance in the world markets. Manufactured goods exports are growing at a rate of 15 percent per annum, and represent over 60 percent of the country's external output. In contrast, prior to trade liberalization, oil exports dominated the external sector, accounting for some 75 percent of the total. Today, oil sales constitute less than 30 percent of sales abroad. Thus, NAFTA provides an opportunity to diversify underdeveloped trade structures as well as to attain higher levels of domestic competitiveness via duty-free market access.

The idea of competitiveness supplies the third fundamental argument for NAFTA in Latin America and the Caribbean. The treaty lays the foundations of competitiveness by providing broad-based rules to allow for long-term planning, access to updated technology, incentives to specialize, and free entry to the largest market in the world.

As a trade arrangement, NAFTA represents a source of increased global competitiveness not just in bringing together the largest trade zone in the world with the highest level of real purchasing power. For Latin America and the Caribbean, it represents an opportunity to develop economies of scale and specialization. The prevalence of trade quotas and other quantitative and technical restrictions in the U.S. and Canadian market inhibits several firms south of the North American border from reducing costs and thus strengthening their competitive position via economies of scale. NAFTA stipulates that 84 percent of Mexican non-oil goods (some 7,000 products) now receive full duty-free and quantitative-free treatment. Similarly, 40 percent of U.S. and Canadian goods are now subject to immediate phase-outs as of the same date. Since this percentage is mostly constituted by high technology and modern equipment, the phase-out norms are able to respect so-called "economic asymmetries." This would apply to all Latin American and Caribbean nations.

A fourth argument for NAFTA is that this accord seeks to meet the capital needs of underdeveloped economies. The 1990s are characteristically an era of acute capital scarcity. Of the total stock of world investment today, only 25 percent is destined to go to the less developed world. For Latin America and the Caribbean, it is imperative to continue attracting a large flow of new capital investments. This is an extra-commercial aspect of the accord, albeit one that is crucially important to the strategy of open trade and its contribution in supplying producers with long-term rules of the economic game.

In effect, regional agreements like NAFTA embody an unnoticed strategic benefit in making countries more competitive in domestic policy. For instance, in Mexico, crucial changes in agrarian law, port and airport privatization, private management of infrastructure, water deregulation, and much more, constitute indirect results of the salutary effects that trade opening has on making domestic economic structures more competitive. In other words, the strategic value of NAFTA lies in its potential for *literally forcing government* to follow trade-consistent policies. This means that a policy which inhibits competitiveness will either tend to disappear, or adapt to change.

The commitment embodied in the Miami Summit to pursue a positive agenda for extending NAFTA everywhere in the continent means that the cause of hemispheric open trade no longer remains a rhetorical possibility but is now a possible reality.

Will the Peso Devaluation Help Exports?

The Zedillo administration has attempted to sell future net gains in increased exports as a long-term benefit of the peso devaluation. So construed, the adjusted value of the peso projected for 1995 (4.5 per U.S. dollar) is supposed to solve the problem of currency overvaluation and give domestic products a competitive edge in the international marketplace. This, together with a more expensive dollar, is also supposed to curb import growth and thereby halt the disproportionate growth of the current account deficit. The crucial questions is: does a cheaper currency constitute a *sufficient condition* to stimulate high export-led economic growth?

The government bets that it can. The new projections for 1995 place the post-devaluation current account deficit at more than half the amount expected before the exchange-rate adjustment: $14 billion U.S., which is equivalent to 4.2 percent of GDP. Total exports are expected to reach 22.6 percent of GDP, spurred by vigorous growth in the manufacturing sector. This is higher than the original pre-devaluation forecast of 17.3 percent. In principle, these estimates reflect the logic of the new orthodoxy that the peso devaluation will increase exports, curb imports and therefore erase a lot of theoretically undesirable red ink in the current account.

The logic is dubious. An important survey conducted by the Centro de Estudios Economicos del Sector Privado (the think-tank of the Business Coordinating Council) prior to the currency devaluation, shows that 80 percent of 450 companies polled across the country believed that the former 4.5 percent depreciation scheme was consistent with higher sales perspectives for 1995. More importantly, the same survey shows that exchange-rate overvaluation ranks seventh in the gamut of factors that domestic companies deem as obstacles to exports. The lack of adequate information on foreign markets and the contraction in demand ranked far higher in this list. Indeed, prior to the devaluation, exports were already growing in the area of 20 percent as a result of trade liberalization and greater market access under NAFTA.

At best, the peso devaluation provides an artificial advantage for exports, not a competitive advantage. According to Deutsche Bank, Mexico could witness a jump of as much as 30 percent in exports in 1995 as a consequence of a depreciated currency, which in cash terms equals an unprecedented $48 billion. This estimate assumes that inflation will remain under control, and this assumption is gratuitous. The majority of private analysts concur that inflation may reach as high as 30 percent, and that despite a welcome annual inflation rate of 7.05 percent for 1994, the days of single-digit inflation are over. If so, it is baseless to claim that devaluation will "help" exports. The short-term gains derived from exchange-rate adjustment are eventually wiped out by the rise in prices, demands for higher wages, sharp increase in interest rates and more expensive capital equipment sorely needed for modernization.

This is exactly what occurred in the wake of the monetary disasters of '76, '82 and '87, and so far the indication is that the government has failed to short-circuit the vicious inflation-devaluation-inflation circle that sharp currency depreciations engender. Indeed, a strong devaluation constitutes a hidden and exceedingly punitive tariff on goods and services. It acts as a roundabout subsidy of exports and thereby inhibits the incentive to modernize, invest in new equipment and compete on the basis of higher quality. The net long-term effect is an external sector with a backward productive infrastructure. So construed, the benefits of exchange-rate modification are overwhelmingly outweighed by the costs.

It is important to note that the problem with the exchange-rate parity prior to the currency collapse was not the existence of a large current account deficit, but the mode in which the deficit was being financed. This represents a problem of the requirements to balance the financial needs of the capital account. True, the currency overvaluation had led to an untenable exchange rate. But the growth in the trade-based current account, estimated at 8 percent of GDP in pre-devaluation estimates, was a natural outcome of trade expansion under NAFTA and greater investment flows associated with the new regime in a foreign investment. Most specialized projections had forecasted a systematic increase in the current deficit to *as much as $35 billion by 1998.*

In light of this, the natural policy to adopt was to place emphasis on fashioning the right conditions to sustain high capital inflows. This entailed initiatives in the form of privatization of state sectors, more deregulation and growth-enhancing tax reform, to neutralize exchange-rate jitters and sustain confidence in the economy. This scenario is required in order to restore confidence and divorce commercial liberalization from the artificial stimulus of exchange-rate manipulation preached by institutions such as the IMF. In exchange-rate matters in Mexico, confidence is everything. An important finding which undermines the thesis of competitiveness gains via the exchange-rate adjustment, is that between 1982 and 1992, the peso suffered over 100 percent devaluation, yet the margin of undervaluation (i.e., real competitiveness) gained in the interim was only 34 percent. the loss of confidence following the 1982 and 1987 devaluations devastated competitiveness. This finding is supported by a recent analysis done by the local bank BANAMEX, which identifies only one rubric among twenty in the manufacturing export-oriented sector (transportation equipment) that will benefit from an adjustment in the current exchange-rate.

Mexico requires a more export-oriented economy. However, this goal is less likely to ensue through a devaluation of the medium of exchange than through hard work in cutting countless regulations, reducing bureaucracy, and ridding the economy of the burden imposed by costly legal and institutional obstacles. Domestic exporters will benefit far more from increased productivity, high-tech equipment and cheaper credit, than from the counterproductive stimulus of devaluation.

In the words of economist Joe Cobb: a country never gets *strong* by *weakening* its currency.

Accountability and Transparency

A lesson of the peso devaluation for Latin American and Caribbean nations is that institutional competitiveness requires a monetary system that is stable, accountable and transparent. The Zedillo administration has characterized the currency debacle as an "inevitable" outcome of a high current account deficit and the negative influence of the political shocks that undermined the financial stability of the economy during 1994. It is a convenient story, since the idea that this latest monetary disaster was the product of forces beyond the presidential reach entails that the current government cannot be held accountable for bringing about such a sharp reduction in the value of the currency.

The issue of exchange-rate adjustment transcends the fancy econometric models fashioned in the ivory towers of Yale, Stanford and MIT. It is an issue which centers on the *medium of exchange* and the *real value* of a person's patrimony. For this reason, future efforts to create a more reliable monetary system must incorporate the normative concepts of *accountability* and *transparency* into the framework governing monetary policy. This would act as a mechanism of checks and balances to maintain the most important ingredient of sustainable economic growth: price stability.

Naturally, this framework was *supposed* to be provided by the strategic impact of NAFTA in locking in the permanence of policies such as responsible monetary policy and fiscal discipline. The implementation of an autonomous regime in the central bank, backed by a constitutional mandate to preserve the purchasing power of the currency, seemed to be a reliable indication that public policy would be consistent with the demands of price and exchange-rate stability. The peso collapse made manifest that an autonomous monetary policy constitutes a verbal commitment void of accountability on the part of Mexico's monetary authorities. Indeed, the latter *have failed to explain if or why* they violated a constitutional mandate to maintain price stability.

Domingo Cavallo, Argentina's finance minister, claims that each unit of currency is an implicit contract between the government and the ordinary holder of currency. This is supposed to guarantee that the value of the currency will remain stable throughout a specified period of time. According to this logic, a devaluation breaks this contract and therefore breaks the law. This normative view of monetary stability has been incorporated into the framework of countries which place a premium on the value of the currency. The best example is New Zealand, where legislation prohibits the central bank from allowing more than 2 percent inflation rates per annum. Similarly, in Argentina, Cavallo himself acted as the main architect of a system which is rapidly gaining a reputation as a reliable mechanism for building and sustaining monetary confidence. This mechanism is called a currency board.

In Argentina, the currency board system helped the country to bring inflation down from quadruple-digit levels to 3 percent in just three years. A new currency replaced the worthless austral and was pegged one-to-one with the U.S. dollar, backed by constitutional law in the form of a convertibility law, which acts as a powerful straitjacket limiting the government's capacity to print money by requiring *that all money in circulation* be fully redeemable by outstanding hard currency reserves.

Mexico seems ripe for such a system. The current state of affairs is more a crisis of *credibility* than a crisis of financial concerns. The latter requires an adjustment in the form of credit lines and payment procedures for items such as tesobono securities and ordinary debt instruments. The former demands shock therapy. According to Steve Hanke, a leading authority on currency boards, the main characteristic of this system is that 'it commands instant credibility." It makes the monetary constitution of a country fully transparent and fully accountable, by imposing an ultra-strict discipline in fiscal and in monetary matters.

The peso devaluation has been met with outrage and with a profound loss of hope on the part of citizens who were told one thing and received another. To avoid such crises in the future, it is necessary to fashion the proper legal mechanisms that can force monetary authorities to be both accountable and transparent to the citizenry at large.

Conclusion

It is essential to divorce the incompetence with which the Zedillo administration has handled exchange-rate policy in Mexico from the potential benefits of hemispheric free trade. In particular, a proper approach to the financial turbulence that has ensued in the wake of the peso crisis requires disassociating the model of NAFTA as a pragmatic instrument of trade expansion from the erroneous monetary decision-making pursued by the Zedillo government. The hope is that future policy discussions retain a clear perspective on the need for open trade.

The Miami agenda represents an outstanding opportunity to consolidate the cause of open trade in the Western hemisphere. In the end, despite the negative precedent set by Mexico in 1994 (one of the most turbulent periods in the nation's modern history), the debates concerning the economic benefits of hemispheric liberalization must heed the simple truth of trade; namely, that when the exchange of goods and services is free and voluntary, everyone necessarily benefits.

Economic Benefits of NAFTA
and Hemispheric Integration (IV)

SIDNEY WEINTRAUB

Congressman Hamilton in his opening remarks gave some deserved praise to the Hudson Institute for its role in trade analysis of NAFTA, GATT, and all the rest. I want to do the same for Michael Walker and the Fraser Institute. This is the second, third, fourth or fifth time I have been affiliated with the Fraser Institute in a conference, and while I knew little about them a few years ago, I know an awful lot now. I think the Institute and Michael have done more to encourage honest-to-goodness economic analyses of integration in the Americas than just about anybody. And for that I congratulate you.

I am going to speak mostly as an economist, I am not going to get too much into politics and whether the U.S. government is ready for the upcoming hemispheric summit in Miami. I think it is.

First, what is the basis for the economic gains, the benefits that will come from the economic integration under NAFTA? I will make three points and then elaborate briefly on these. One is the question of the certainty of rules. This is a point that Roberto Salinas made. It is an important point. During the debate on NAFTA, one of the arguments made against the agreement was that since U.S. tariffs

Sidney Weintraub is Dean Rusk Professor at the Lyndon B. Johnson School of Public Affairs, University of Texas at Austin and holds the William E. Simon Chair in Political Economy, Center for Strategic and International Studies.

are low anyhow, and the U.S. has few non-tariff barriers—why did we need the elaborate NAFTA structure? Two countries were silently integrating: Why did we need an agreement to formalize what was happening anyhow? The answer is that we needed an agreement to formalize what was happening so we would have certainty about the future, to assume that these things would not be temporary but would go from administration to administration. The day after his inauguration, President Zedillo had a luncheon for various business people and other visitors. Both Riordan Roett and I were there. One of the things he said to the congregated group was: "I want you to take one word above all others away with you when you leave here, and that word is stability." I think that is an important point explaining the rationale behind NAFTA.

Two, the long-term benefits of the integration under NAFTA will come from its deepening. The fact that tariffs will be low matters somewhat—but not anywhere near as much as the other kinds of deepening that may accompany NAFTA. Not just NAFTA, but NAFTA and beyond, and by beyond I mean integration of the hemisphere. I'll come back to that point briefly in a few moments.

And finally, the most important point is the ability of business people—producers and providers of services—to treat the region as a single production area and as a single market. Plans can now be made with that in mind and that, combined with the theme of stability, is really what we are talking about when we talk about regional integration.

What do I mean by deepening? The most important aspect of deepening, it seems to me, is going to be the harmonization of industrial production and other standards necessary for the conduct of production and trade. It is relatively easy to harmonize standards within the same firm but it is much harder across firms. They include standards for the movement of trains and trucks; for financial services. Europe '92, the European Community's earlier program, dealt mainly with this issue. Harmonization will not be possible across the board, and in some areas we may have to adopt what the Europeans did using the principle of mutual acceptance of each other's standards. It will probably not be possible to harmonize environmental standards, but we should be able to upgrade them.

All of us in the trade business have long known that one could write an industrial standard to exclude foreign products. The United States did this for boilers for many, many years. One can write a sanitary standard—we still do it for avocados—which can keep out foreign goods.

Harmonization and mutual acceptance are the essence of deepening. Without that, no matter what the tariffs are, there will not be tremendous benefits. In addition, countries write regulations all the time. One aspect of deepening is the ability to penetrate the regulatory writing process of each one of the other countries to be able to get in early to say, 'No this won't do."We all know—especially those of us in governments who have learned how to do these things—we know how to write regulations that will make sure that national products get benefits and the other guy's products don't get benefits. We just did it at the insistence of the Congress with respect to Venezuelan oil and oxygenation, for which the U.S. will be taken to the GATT or the World Trade Organization. It's that kind of discriminatory regulation writing that we must try to prevent in a regional integration arrangement.

Finally, deepening means something that Jules Katz referred to—improving the rules of origin, making them less restrictive some way or another. Where possible we can convert the tariffs we now have into a common external tariff for which rules of origin are no longer necessary. As Jules said, we have already done this in the computer industry, and there is really no reason not to do this more extensively as NAFTA deepens.

Let me give just a few examples of some recent restrictive actions. I will give one from each country.

Mexico not too long ago changed its labeling rules so that you couldn't use stickers on goods like computers coming in. The origin of the product had to be labeled in Spanish on the product itself. The change had to be done from one night to the next morning, when nobody could have managed to accomplish it. There was no reason for the hurry other than to keep out some U.S. products.

The Canadians are debating extension of some of their cultural industry exceptions—relating even to country music. This is not being done just to protect culture, because country music is hardly

Canadian culture. There are limits on advertising that reduce reader-ship of U.S. publications, particularly magazines. Canadians could subsidize their publications, but they prefer the more restrictive way.

In the United States, we have become extremely innovative in using anti-dumping duties. We use them to a fare-thee-well to make sure that we keep out products from Canada, Mexico, and the rest of the world.

These things happen. They are not the essence of what is go-ing on in North America, but they are illustrative. When the transpar-ent import barriers go down, people start using other barriers; and when governments permit this, they can destroy the essence of integration. Integration means that such protectionist devices will slowly have to go the way of the dinosaur. This won't happen over-night, but I am confident that these occult trade barriers will disap-pear eventually.

Let me make one or two other points. One, on the measure-ment of benefits. Ex ante, before NAFTA came into effect, a lot of us did all kinds of measurements of what the benefits would be. I am normally at the University of Texas at Austin. We did a model as to how Texas would benefit from NAFTA. Texas by the way is by far the biggest exporting state to Mexico. Most U.S. goods pass through Texas and a substantial part of the goods that go to Mexico are produced in Texas. Texas has a lot at stake in the success of NAFTA. We made some projections about Texas exports to Mexico. We were essentially right except we understated dramatically. The growth in exports was much, much bigger than we had estimated.

I have looked at many other projections—the computable general equilibrium models, some of the econometric models, including even the historical model which Jeff Schott was associated with. All had the signs right, but just about all understated the growth in trade, at least in the first year.

What we all left out was the excitement effect that NAFTA brought about, both in the United States and in Canada toward Mex-ico, and in Mexico toward the other two countries. You see this excitement if you visit Mexico. The hotels are full of foreign-ers—everybody wants to get in on the act. One of my tourist agent friends told me that the good hotels in Mexico are now 95 percent plus booked during the week. Don't go to Mexico without a reservation if you want to get into a good hotel.

Canada and Mexico have discovered each other. The percentage growth in their exports to each other far surpasses what's happening in U.S.-Mexico trade. From a lower level, it's true, but the discovery is real. This wouldn't have happened without NAFTA.

I get calls daily from business people about NAFTA. I have been associated with Mexico for a long time and I keep hearing from people who have now discovered the place. The rising trade, the benefits, have been much more enormous than we expected. It's only one year, the time is short, but still the trade expansion has more than met the test of the proponents of NAFTA. I couldn't agree more with what Alan Reynolds said—the test is not the trade surplus or trade deficit any one of us has, but rather the two-way increase and two-way trade that takes place. That's the real measurement of the benefit of agreements like NAFTA.

We are now beginning to see rationalization of production and of marketing. Much co-production that is taking place under which components of a product are produced in many places and then assembled at perhaps still another place. This is happening for products across the board. The amount of trade taking place *intra-firm* is growing. Canadian exports of manufactured goods to the U.S. are now 60 percent plus intra-firm. The same firm is producing parts of goods in the two countries. Intra-firm trade is now in excess of 50 percent for Mexican exports of manufactured goods to the U.S. These are the kinds of things that one must look at when studying integration areas.

I'll say just a few words about the expansion of free trade in the hemisphere. I think expansion is desirable and I think it's time to get moving. I think accession of Chile is more than symbolic. While it is a small country, Chile can become the model—the expression and the realization of what we've promised since 1990. If Chile enters under terms that meet the provisions of NAFTA, that protect the deepening, I think we will see a lot more coming in after Chile on similar terms. Thus I think the Chile case is really quite important and I would applaud the administration for its plan to go ahead with Chile.

Eventually, I want to subsume all of Mexico's bilaterals into NAFTA. I think what Mexico has done is create the spaghetti that Jules Katz referred to more than anybody else. It's time the spaghetti making stopped. I don't want to expand NAFTA to other countries if this weakens the deepening I talked about. In other words, my view is that a country should not be admitted unless it can meet the obligations that exist in the Agreement. For weaker countries, I would much prefer partial agreements—these can take the form of an interim agreement for the Caribbean Basin countries, or an investment agreement, or intellectual property agreements, and opening of financial market agreements. There are many ways to reach agreements for countries not yet ready to take on the fuller obligations of NAFTA without complicating the deepening of NAFTA and the widening of free trade in the hemisphere.

One comment on regional integration of Latin America which I think is important because of the philosophy it represents. I think that Mercosur can be even worse than Jules said. Mercosur is a customs union in which barriers will be kept high on some critical products. Jules mentioned computers. This can mean that the weaker countries, not just Argentina but Paraguay and Uruguay may have to pay more for these products because they can't buy them in the world markets at world prices. This is exactly what destroyed the integration effort in Latin America in the 1960s. I don't think this is a trivial issue. I have little good to say about integration that increases protection.

Both Congressmen Hamilton and Jules Katz referred to the need to overcome protectionist sentiment by education and I agree with them. Yet those of us who have been in the trade business for very long, have learned that we can prevail in liberalizing trade. I wouldn't be as pessimistic as other speakers have been. Over the years, since the Franklin Roosevelt administration, progress in trade liberalization has been quite steady. In other words, I don't think we should treat the U.S., Mexican, and Canadian publics as a bunch of yahoos. I think they are able to grasp the issues.

Democracy and Free Trade in the Western Hemisphere

SENATOR RICHARD G. LUGAR

I am very grateful to the co-sponsors of this meeting—Hudson Institute and the Fraser Institute—and to each one of you who have come to the Hoosier capitol for a very important conference. This educational opportunity will hopefully propagate the faith that the expansion of world trade is an important interest of our country.

My thoughts today will be directed toward economic integration and the strengthening of democracy in the hemisphere. But I want to start by discussing our democracy—politics in this country—particularly in the area of trade, as the President and others from his administration go to the Miami Summit later this week. This has to be a major focus for us.

We have in the last few days been through the tortures of the GATT debate and votes—the cobbling together of majorities that were large in both the House and the Senate, on both the final votes and, in the case of the Senate, on the procedural budget question. I must tell you that one reason why those votes took an extended session was the uncertainty on the part of the Administration and

Senator Richard G. Lugar, the Chairman of the Senate Agriculture Committee, became Indiana's first four-term U.S. Senator in January 1995.

Congressional leadership during the regular session as to whether the job could be done at all.

The specifics of getting the 60 votes for the budget waiver have brought criticism on the Administration for putting us in that predicament. It also brought a certain censure on all who were debating the issue, for their failure to grasp what the whole proposition was really about. In short, we were in a predicament in which some people were seriously offering the proposition that the cut of tariffs in our country and around the world would lead to a reduction of revenue for our government. Indeed, that reduction was extrapolated for one year, five years or ten years, as if the amount of trade that is going to occur would be static. That this should prove to be a point on which the entire agreement to expand trade, income and jobs could have faltered was bizarre. But it was utilized by persons who still have traces of protectionism in their political outlook.

The predicament we face—whether at the Miami Summit, or in extending NAFTA to Chile or beginning a serious dialogue with other countries—is the fact that the fast track mechanism still has a very uncertain future. The Chileans—who I am told the President will approach at Miami—virtually have to accept on faith that we will get our situation straightened out after discussions are underway.

It is our democracy, really, which is the source of doubt in this particular case—not theirs. We have simply been through this too many times now with the NAFTA and the GATT debates. A very significant number of our countrymen argued that these are bad propositions. Bad in the sense that American jobs are going to be lost, that America's technical know-how may be dissipated, and, in the case of the GATT, that the World Trade Organization, which our nation had proposed for all these years, might lead to the subordination of U.S. interests. Everyone is now looking for escape hatches, and some are wishing that the six months' notice for leaving the WTO could be shortened.

On that uncertain terrain, the Miami Summit begins. Some columnists who are interested in sensationalism have argued that Miami is perhaps not the best place to have it. I think Governor Chiles would disagree and so would many people throughout the hemisphere. Miami is a robust center of a great deal of trade and tourism. It's true that the ethnicity of the city affects our democracy. It clearly affected our immigration policy during the last campaign. The facts of life are that, in my judgment, the Clinton Administration, with the heavy prodding of Governor Chiles, backed almost instantly by the Attorney General of the United States, decided to change immigration policy. The aftermath of that decision is the presence of large numbers of Cuban refugees still in Guantanamo, though that situation is being alleviated for children and those who are in great difficulty. It is not really clear how, if we are dealing with democracy, we deal with Cuba, with Haiti, or even with a country such as Colombia that has a different set of problems, which were brought to my attention by its distinguished ambassador the other day. Those are the problems of our relations with a country that has very severe narcotrafficking problems that we have been trying to solve.

I want to add a further thought at the outset—that from the beginning of the debates on NAFTA and GATT there has been a presumption by many members of the House and Senate (and perhaps even more vividly by the public as a whole) that foreign policy issues were not of great interest to us. Those of us in public life are regaled with stories all of the time about what a very small percentage of people care about foreign policy. On the hustings I am reminded of this as if I somehow do not understand it. It is almost an article of faith or theology—that the people are uninterested in these issues and that, therefore, I should be as well. That in a democracy we ought to pay attention only to those things that are the most important. From the debate of 1992 and the presidential campaign onward, the idea was "the economy, stupid." Without laying all the blame upon President Clinton, there were many Republicans who said the Cold War is over and George Bush in that election campaign ought to have been much more preoccupied with a domestic game plan or to have explained what he was doing since that was the focus of interest. As a matter of fact, that is where our debate has been. We've spent our time on health care in this country and its reform. There was a glimmering that welfare reform was coming along, but even that was delayed by preoccupation with medical reform. We discussed the budget and spending and taxes for some time, and we tried to cap spending, raise taxes and do something with the budget deficit. That clearly fit the mold of being concerned about ourselves here in this country.

Those were critical issues. I don't deny it, and I've been discussing those issues. But it is conceivable that you can do two things at once—that is, handle the domestic situation and foreign affairs. It is ironic, and I don't wish to make more problems for the President, that in the final two weeks of the campaign when the President went to the Middle East, he had some rise in his ratings. It was when he came home, preoccupied with domestic affairs, that things went crashing down again. I think that in his heart of hearts, judging by conversations that I have had with this President—and they have been more extended in terms of length and subject matter than with any President—he is deeply involved in these questions. With regard to NAFTA and GATT, his own leadership—galvanizing all the people he could bring into his orbit—was critical to the final passage of both. In the final two years of this first term of President Clinton—undoubtedly he will be a candidate again—it is important that he offer presidential leadership.

When Secretary of State Christopher asked me to have breakfast last Tuesday, I leapt at the opportunity. The first thing I discussed, knowing that I was going to be with you today, was the Miami Summit, and I sought some assurance about our position. To be very candid, I said, 'I hope, you've gotten over the labor business and the environment business. Not that these are unimportant issues. But the key issue is free trade in the hemisphere, and how we are going to get on with that." And Secretary Christopher replied that trade is the preeminent issue. There will be a paragraph or two referring to labor issues and to the environment, as there should be, but probably no date, probably no particular framework that might change our negotiating position—I leave that to his judgment. My own view about this is that I hope that might change in the process of evaluation. The fact is, it is critically important for the United States to accelerate the various international agreements—I am told there are 23 of these in some form in our hemisphere now—that will require reconciliation and a lot of working groups to bring together. We will need to find the points that are inconsistent in some way with our laws and with their laws. But the fact is that even after you talk about the working groups, it is the political will and the interests of our country that are of primary importance in Miami.

The Miami Summit comes at a time when many of our Latin American friends say we have turned our back on them, or are less interested in them, or our enthusiasm is suspect, or we've kept them waiting a long time. The Chileans are a case in point. We have been pushing an agenda as we saw it, not as they saw it. We have not been listening to them, they say. They say they are patient but are moving on their own. Some groups in Chile, not in the government, even say that 41 percent of their trade is already with the Mercosur group, that we have already missed the boat, but that it's still possible for the United States to get aboard. We, on the other hand, tend to look at it as gratuitous, that we might help out the Chileans. Now they still have a very small economy. We have a very large one. But Mercosur is getting bigger, and so are other arrangements that leave us out. Our lack of attention to all this—whether it be lack of attention from the Congress or the administration—doesn't alter the fact that the world continues to turn. Other nations from outside our hemisphere have become very interested in the trading opportunities here. They are suddenly much more active players. So as we go to Miami, after we indicate that we care, that we are very much in the ball game to accelerate free trade, I hope that we also say—and mean it—that we are sensitive, we're listening, we're hearing and we're prepared to act upon many of the suggestions of the friends we will find there.

Now, let me just say that the Indiana Farm Bureau has been meeting next door this week. I have been talking to many friends there, first of all about the GATT. Indiana Farm Bureau, of all the statewide groups here, was the first and most enthusiastic group to come out for NAFTA. They were an essential part of that coalition, because the attitude at the grass roots of this state was suspicious about free trade. Not so with the Farm Bureau. From the beginning, they correctly assessed that agriculture in this state, in this country, would thrive if those trade barriers in Mexico were reduced. They were absolutely right. There is no doubt in the minds of any of the delegates there that this was the right call from the beginning. They were also among the first to come out strongly for GATT. Now, that's a tougher sell. The Farm Bureau members listened to talk radio and various other discussions of the World Trade Organization just as other people do. As I was visiting with them last evening, many said they were glad GATT passed, but raised questions about the WTO. What about that secret group meeting of 140 nations? How about our sovereignty? Are you going to look out for us? So even with GATT passed, seeds of doubt have been sowed, even among the group I found to be the most ardent supporter from the very beginning.

Now when we get to the farm bill, which we have also been discussing this week, we'll encounter such things as our sugar program. The sugar program from an economic standpoint is a terrible thing. I can not say enough bad about it. It is a travesty that in this country we would try to protect producers of sugar in Florida and in Louisiana and the Dakotas. We protect every one of them. That is the policy—to have a sugar price so high that every single person producing sugar in this country can make a living at it, even though most of them could not compete in the world market. That is just one of the manifestations of our farm bill.

Five years ago when we last discussed the farm bill, I introduced an amendment to abolish the sugar program. It got one other vote in committee, and that Senator, for the sake of his reputation shall remain nameless because he is still in the Senate. Even as we discussed GATT, many people in agricultural America shuffled around and said, 'Now, it's really the French and the Europeans who are the malefactors. We have already reduced our subsidies so far that we can satisfy the required domestic subsidy cuts during the first six years without taking any further action." They're looking for reassurance that we can get away with keeping target prices, loan rates, deficiency payments and the program crops and the other smaller subsidies. Maybe so, but clearly the spirit of GATT, the spirit of NAFTA, and I hope now the spirit of citizens is that we ought to begin to dismantle the subsidies that were put in place during the New Deal in the 1930s and have been built upon ever since.

One of the great ironies is that even the New Deal did not do to agriculture what the last decade has done. If you look at the amount of spending on agriculture, you see a long line of inflation-adjusted expenditures of between $1 billion and $4 billion up through the 1970s. And then things literally went wild. We had a year of $26 billion, punctuated by a year of $17 billion. As I pointed out to the delegates last night, we aimed in 1990 at $51 billion in subsidies just in the four crops—cotton, rice, corn and wheat—for the last five years. The Budget Summit of 1990 cut the $51 to $41 billion, but in reality we have spent $57 billion. You ask, how can this be? It can be very easily. It's an entitlement. Farm spending has similar characteristics to all other entitlements.

This really won't help free trade arrangements in Miami. I am not certain it will really work for our budget debate either. We are about to come to a crucial point in January. In the midst of all of the discussions on priorities, the balanced budget amendment will come up early. Pete Domenici and John Kasich and others who have new responsibility for the budget point out that our entitlements, if left to run as is, will consume 85 percent of the budget in the year 2002, leaving just 15 percent for all the other things for which Congress appropriates. People in Latin America are reading those pie charts the same as some of us; it sobers everybody up. It doesn't mean that the balanced budget amendment by 2002 isn't going to be passed. I think it will pass. Whether it will go through the states may be more problematic. But we are in for a change. Many of you have written papers for this conference and say that we have to show some fiscal responsibility. The problem of capital shortage in this country, in the hemisphere, and in the world can't very well be solved with the leader in a non-saving attitude.

The point I want to emphasize is that in our farm bill, in our budgetary process this year, we need to do some things that are very constructive, that are perceived that way, and that offer hope to our friends and negotiators that we have a constructive international outlook. Stopping the sugar protection would be not only symbolic but indicative of good faith, because the enrichment of the hemisphere—in terms of competitive imports and exports—is extremely meaningful. And while I'm on that subject, I would say that we ought to examine in this country the Export Enhancement Program. The EEP was a set of agriculture subsidies designed to fire shots across the bow of the French and others who we felt were dumping their highly subsidized wheat and other products. They will continue to do that, I suspect, but we have spent during the last year as much as $8 billion to boost our agriculture exports. Just our agriculture exports alone. Some of that we will get back from GSM loans and some we won't. The expenses of the EEP program will be entirely written off. This is a way of reducing the price of wheat to rock bottom until you finally get the sale and make certain it is not taken away by somebody who is dumping right along with you. Once again all of our friends in Miami are aware of that. It doesn't hit them quite so hard because we have not aimed at them. But our friends in Australia routinely complain about this, as do others who take free trade in agriculture seriously.

In addition to the problems of free trade, we also have the special case of Haiti. Some administration people with whom I've visited prior to the Miami conference have said we ought to highlight what we have done in Haiti as an example of how a democracy can be furthered. Let me make a case for that point of view for a moment, because my own strong views prior to the present intervention in Haiti were that we ought not to intervene. But let me just say that the work of our armed forces there, and the work of the administration with President Aristide and others in the Haitian leadership has led to a situation where they have a great deal more hope for themselves and for their future. The presence of United States military forces and the semblance of order and stability that they have brought has made a very large difference. President Aristide has reached out to the business community and to people who have been his political enemies—and that understates it—to get them interested in the future. He is still embattled, protected really by our military power. It's also proving very difficult to get the elections underway. I saw six members of the Haitian legislature in Washington last week who were opponents of Aristide. That was an important experience, to hear six articulate legislators who would be much more vital if, in fact, the legislature worked and there were checks and balances, a free press and freedom of expression. But as many have said, in Haiti we are starting from ground zero. There are very few institutions to latch onto. The question from the beginning with regard to intervention was how long we were prepared to stay, how much responsibility our country was prepared to assume for that government in the intermediate period, maybe even in the long run. I think the jury is still out. Another conference might even be held on what you do if you go into a country and really try to build a democracy, an economy, and new customs from scratch. Now to an extent that is not our intent, and from time to time the President and the military authorities say that is not our intent. As a matter of fact a lot of troops will be out by Christmas, and more troops out in early 1995. A UN peacekeeping force or some type of group will be replacing them with some U.S. troops still standing by. It's difficult to know exactly how that will go. Will the United Nations, with diffuse voices, have the same views on democracy and development that the United States does? Right now it is our responsibility, our voices and thoughts. We frankly don't know whether people are lying in wait for the United States to leave before they do their devilment.

If Haiti is difficult, Cuba is even more so. I accept the fact that in Miami, the state of Florida and in southern Florida, there are now many voices on the Cuban issue. The political assumption used to be that people who had left Cuba were of one mind, and the one mind was to oppose Castro until he dies, wears down, or gives up the ghost. Many people still harbor the idea. Give no quarter, squeeze harder, and if he hasn't dropped, squeeze harder still. Perhaps he will. But if he doesn't, then we have problems like those we had last summer when in the middle of a Florida election campaign the Cubans went to sea. Governor Chiles called the White House and Janet Reno responded on CNN—at a very late hour of the night—reformulating U.S. immigration policy. But she was right on track with what the administration saw needed to be done; namely, stop the Cubans as quickly as possible, not far out to sea, but right off the shores. Get them to Guantanamo, and keep them there until we decide what to do. Most are still there. Haitians, it is pointed out, now having a democracy, or a semblance of democracy, are free to go home, and some are leaving. About half are still there.

In the meantime we have had a debate on Proposition 187 in California in which 59 percent of voting Californians tried to make a statement about illegal immigration. Governor Wilson tried to make a statement on this. Many Americans believe the statement that was made lacks constitutionality and is too complex to enforce. But it doesn't mean that the issue is over. The issue of immigration is a very important one in this country, because many Americans feel that things may have gotten out of hand. The INS really doesn't have control of the borders and hasn't had control for a long time. We really don't know what is occurring in the southwest part of our country or in our large urban areas as people immigrate. This creates other issues that weren't expected. Certainly Salvadorans hadn't expected to get into the argument. Yet there they were in the *Washington Post*, because the Washington metropolitan area has a large number of Salvadorans who have come to the United States, remitting back to El Salvador more money than all of their leading exports generated. El Salvador was once a very important foreign policy issue for us. It hasn't been for a while; we had lost track of El Salvador until we got into the immigration issue last week. Now we find that hundreds of thousands of Salvadorans are in our country having outlived their legal stay and in threat of deportation. It's cold comfort to them that the deportation system of this country works so haltingly that it could be years before they are found and notified.

I mention this because the Mexicans are very exercised about immigration issues. The critical point about the Miami summit and about our relations with Mexico is that we were asked by the Mexicans to take up the NAFTA debate. I was telling those at our table about my first trip to Mexico on a Congressional delegation. I went with Senator Lloyd Bentsen and Representative Jim Wright, both of whom spoke Spanish and were able to arrange meetings with the highest circles. We had a fairly good idea of the feelings people had in those days. During the last administration, the Salinas administration issued an invitation to us on forming a free trade area that we could not refuse, and thank goodness did not. At the same time we are trying to help democracy and offering free advice on how to reform, the immigration situation we've thrown up with Proposition 187 unfortunately makes life very difficult for them.

Recently, the Colombian Ambassador made the point to me that we will have to decide whether we want to work with them in the anti-narcotic effort. The same could be said for the Peruvians and the Bolivians. The Ambassador said it is very difficult for a Colombian to enter an office or a meeting without people suspecting that somebody dealing in the drug trade has just entered the room. The discussion might be compromised by the very presence of the person. Now, a lot of brilliant young Colombians have come into a new administration. Former Colombian President Gaviria is heading up OAS and offering brilliant leadership. But it's still a very great predicament for Colombia.

One of the papers prepared for this conference stressed that when we are talking about democracy, we are talking, in addition to free and fair elections, about a free and fair judiciary, or at least an independent judiciary. It's tough going in Colombia. It's perilous to run for President in the country and very perilous day in and day out to serve as a judge. We in this country would like to change all that. We would like to buttress the judiciary and get fair election laws adopted with the same zeal that we have been talking about child labor and environment in this administration. I hope in the softer hours at Miami there will be time to listen to those who are fighting the good fight within those countries for democratic ideals and how we could be more effective in our assistance.

Our effectiveness often is gauged by how tough the amendments are to the foreign aid bill when it comes before the Foreign Relations Committee. Most of our foreign aid debates are followed avidly by others in our hemisphere, even though they usually amount to nothing. The Congress has not passed a foreign assistance authorization bill for the last eight years. The appropriators pick up the strings and continue what we did last year plus or minus a few percentages, lopping off funds that may be distressful to one of the members, usually doing this in the dead of the night.

Others recognize that our democratic processes when dealing with foreign aid are suspect. The argument never seems to be centered. The votes never seem to occur, and follow through is suspect, as funds are rearranged by the administration, operating under so many constraints that great ingenuity is required to get the job done. That won't work the same way, one hopes, in the 104th Congress. There will be changes in this, but I'm not overconfident. I would just say that most of the preoccupation in Miami once again has to be about how we run our affairs. This is quite apart from the fact that most Americans don't want to spend money on foreign assistance at all. And if you want to spend a dime, you are confronted by endless polls that show that you are on the wrong side of history.

Several years ago, I was impressed when the great Peruvian novelist and presidential candidate Mario Vargas Llosa spoke in Washington. I was privileged one evening to hear him discuss his philosophy and thoughts about democracy. I made some notes of that experience, because what he had to say, while perhaps not original, was very profound in the context of his discussion of Peruvian democracy. One thing he said was that there had been three straight Peruvian presidencies that went their full course with successors elected. In private, Vargas Llosa was not very generous about the quality of those Peruvian presidencies. He felt in various ways all had been failures. But the fact was that they managed to make it through four years and pass on the baton.

The point he was making is that democracy takes time for the roots to take hold, for the institutions in the country to interact with each other and to take on different form. If you don't have that duration in time, no amount of good will and urgency is likely to get the job done. It was an interesting thought. He made another comment that struck me as the thought of a novelist and keen observer of our hemisphere. He said there is in the Latin psychology an ardent desire for freedom. He said that may be true of other cultures, but he was aware of his, and given a choice, even a person of very little education, or with very little background in the ways of the world, will choose the option that appears to give more freedom.

He said this is why democracy works even in elections such as the one I observed in Guatemala in 1985. President Reagan asked me to head a delegation to go to that country for what had been a very difficult experience. Secretary of State Shultz had asked me to go earlier in the year just to assure General Mejia that we wanted him to cede authority to an election process. The General pointed out how all the oil supplies and money were running out, and there were all sorts of problems. But he did stay the course. The election occurred. I found in the hills of Guatemala that over 50 percent of the electorate were considered illiterate. This was not the first time such an election has been held in such a country, but it was interesting to watch how they did it. They wanted to do it the American way, because they wanted our validation. They wanted our registration methods, and we furnished technical assistance for this election.

Even so, there were real problems. I remember back in the mountains watching a very old lady standing in line for a long time. When it came time to vote, she could not read the instructions. Her language skills were not sufficient to know exactly what she was supposed to do with the ballot—whether to fold it, where to put it, and so forth. People were so fastidious in carrying out their duties that no one told her how to do it for fear that they would be charged with election fraud. After all was said and done, a president was elected and President Cerezo came to the United States within three weeks, met with the Foreign Relations committee and somebody candidly asked him, 'How much authority do you really think you have in Guatemala?" He said, "Well let me express it as a percentage. Maybe 30 percent." And the questioner asked, "Where is the rest of it, if you're not in charge?" He ticked off a whole lot of people, starting with the military, with aristocratic families and various other power brokers who were still around. He indicated, much as Vargas Llosa had said, that you start with a little bit of space.

I make that point because that kind of understanding of the process is tremendously important. The Guatemalans came to us and wanted to know how to run a legislature. The Center for Democracy, the National Endowment for Democracy and others have been furnishing that sort of information and expertise, for a long time. This is critically important. And trade must be central, too. Even after we work out the mechanics and the spirit of how this freedom could be manifested, a democratic government has to produce something, just as our democratic government must. We take it as axiomatic that each election is finally determined on the perceptions of people of their domestic job situation and their sense of security. And so it is with many other democracies, including those very close to us. The overall strategy has been right—trade will increase in our hemisphere if we knock down the barriers. But the fears in this country are still there, as they are in many countries—that if you knock down the barriers, those who have been protected will not be protected and will have to compete and in some cases will lose.

As happy as I am about approval of GATT and NAFTA, I am cognizant that many people in protected niches of agriculture and manufacturing are going to be hurt. If that is true in a county as wealthy as ours, with all the support systems for individuals, it is manifestly true in many other countries with whom we must deal. It comes down to a moment in history where there is a window that might not forever be open.

I can recall in Brazil 10 years ago hearing that foreign investment was an issue on which we had to tread very carefully. I asked someone there: "Do you mean if you could get a $5 billion investment, you wouldn't be willing to sell your utilities?" And I was told, "not on your life. Never more than 49 percent ownership and probably not more than 25 percent. You've got to understand the history of exploitation, others coming in, buying up our resources, and buying up the centers of our communities. We are not going to allow that, now or forever." Today, many people are seriously working to attract American investment. They understand that capital is short around the world, and if they are not receptive to it, it will be invested elsewhere.

Recognition of that fact represents a revolution of sorts, though one that you cannot count upon in other countries or in this one indefinitely. This is the time to prove the case. I hope that Miami will advance it, and I feel confident that it will. Quite apart from halting starts, an uncertain agenda, and a lack of sensitivity and rapport, I think it will be productive. It may be that the GATT debate will generate momentum. That will be useful all by itself. In any event, the most useful aspect will be the advocacy of those of you in the room and others with whom you are allied. In a democracy, ultimately you have to win votes and support. An elite will not be able to fashion this alone, but those who do have strong views and can articulate them can help significantly.

I thank you very much for the honor of giving me this opportunity to address you at this forum.

Next Steps in Expanding NAFTA and Building Hemispheric Economic Integration: The View from Canada and the U.S. (I)

DAVID MALPASS

I am going to talk a little about trade philosophy. I want to give some facts, some observations about free trade, some free trade theory, and make a proposal at the end. Because part of the context of my arguments is going to be negative with regard to free trade agreements, I need to qualify myself a little. I worked hard on the Canada Free Trade Agreement, on the North America Free Trade Agreement, on GATT for many years with the United States government. I supported their passage before the United States Congress. However, I think today we need to really step back a moment before we plunge on to the next step. Let's think about where we are going and what our objectives are, where we should head for the future.

First I'll state some facts as I understand them with regard to the hemispheric summit. I understand they are going to talk about three groups of issues: economic and trade issues, environmental issues and political issues. They will likely agree to a negotiating deadline of the year 2005 for a free trade agreement of the Americas. The plan of action, as I understand it, has 142 items on it now, one of which is trade. But there are many other items, including corruption, drug trafficking, AIDS, empowerment of women, inter-American disabilities, and so on down the list of interesting items for Latin America to work with the United States on. Clinton will make a

David Malpass is Senior Managing Director, Bear Stearns & Co.

presidential declaration. While it's nice for governments to talk with one another, it seems to me they are way off track with regard to heading forward for the good of the United States and Latin America. A lot of what Latin America needs from the United States is wisdom and support in areas other than trade now. To have the Summit lead off with trade and make the assumption that the agenda for the '90s and for the 2000s is the same as the one for the 1980s is presumptuous and I don't think correct.

Now, some facts on the United States relevant to this discussion. Fast track itself has expired or will have expired by the end of 1994. There is no legal requirement for Congress to be given advance notice of future negotiations. As a practical matter, however, it's going to be nearly impossible for the administration to undertake a negotiation with Chile without first having had a signal from Congress of its intention to give fast track. So a lot of what's going on now is people leaping to the next step without really having the administrative ability to get there.

Now, I have a series of observations. First, there are more important items on trade than having more trade agreements. If we think about what's in the United States's interest, what's our primary trade policy goal, it certainly would not be to create more trade agreements. For example, we might decide that it is more important to tariffy the existing quotas. Senator Lugar just mentioned the sugar quota and the difficulty of changing it. The sugar quota is a highly distortive, costly affair for the United States, and yet it is unlikely that it's going to be touched or talked about as Western Hemisphere leaders get together.

The second observation is that fast track, we might as well admit, is dead. The idea of fast-track authority was an idea for the 1980s. Its time came and it was successful in getting GATT and NAFTA done, and it is now gone. For Chile it died in May 1992, I think, when President Aylwin visited the United States and was not granted fast-track authority at that time. It is going to be, I think, nearly impossible to resurrect that transfer to the executive branch of authority from the U.S. Congress, regardless of which party is in control. Fast-track authorization will be fully amendable, and will therefore probably not get done.

A third observation: We have trade negotiators and trade negotiations going on constantly now with tens of thousands of lawyers, lobbyists and the negotiators themselves all working together. Let's not go on the assumption that that is the way it's supposed to be. Remember that's a second best idea in trade. The best idea would be simply to have more open borders for all parties involved. We have gotten now into this idea of the need to have 10,000 pages of text in order to really understand free trade. And it's clear that we are not going on the right track in getting toward free trade. Simply to have a negotiation implies that there is a win-lose prospect that somebody needs to negotiate against someone else. And that gets you started completely away from where you are trying to head with free trade.

Let's also not be misled by the hype of selling free trade agreements. It's clear that once you embark on a free trade agreement negotiation, you have to then focus on all the wonderful things that negotiation is going to bring in order to sell it. But that doesn't mean that that's necessarily the truth about all of the benefits or that we would not be able to get the benefits more easily in another manner. If we look at free trade negotiations, oftentimes they are ratifying something that's already happened. This was true of the European Community, and of NAFTA itself, where Mexico had been working towards free trade for four years before really embarking on NAFTA. And if you look at trade and investment with Mexico, they were actually slowed. This was particularly true of investment, where Mexico lost a good deal of investment in 1993 that was pushed into 1994, because business people were worried about a negative vote on NAFTA. So if you look at Mexico's overall growth rate, at least in the short run, it was probably slowed down by the politicization of NAFTA itself.

A final observation in this list. Putting future dates on trade agreements is a really bad practice. If we put out this date that by 2005 we're going to have a negotiation done with Latin America, there are going to be a lot of business people who make the decision that they should wait until 2005 to make their big investment in Latin America. They will want to see what the exact rules of the game are going to be. So by laying out a future date and a long process, we may very well be slowing down the free trade process that we are trying to get. It would be like the conservative issue of a capital gains tax cut, which is a necessity and something that should be done very quickly. If we proposed the idea of having a negotiation over a capital gains tax cut that was going to come to an end in 1999, it would deepen the problem of the tax lock-in effect. No one would want to sell their stock because they would want to wait to see if they were going to get a lower rate later. That same process may slow down investment activity in Latin America.

So I have a short list of trade theories that I think we need to really settle on and use. One is transparency. We have got to have everyone know what the rules are. Rather than talking about a lot of intricate trade agreements that obscure the trade regime, it would be better to have very simple rules. If it's more than a few pages long, it's probably not a useful free trade agreement.

A second trade principle that we should put more emphasis on is low tariff rates across the board. The best kind of import regime is what Chile does. A 9 percent tax across the board. When you have differential tariffs, which is the norm for Latin America, it is extremely distortive. The rules of the game right now are not transparent. They are distortive. They embody a great deal of costs in terms of the lawyers, lobbyists, and trade negotiators. A proper U.S. goal for free trade, rather than getting a lot more free trade agreements, would be to settle right at the beginning on an objective of finding a political way in the United States to have a very flat tariff across the board on all items. Let us get rid of our own Himalayan tariffs. I think from a theoretical standpoint that would be very successful. That would be a great idea. Let's do it. But politically there is no chance of that. In fact they are now admitting right up front, that there is no way we can get NAFTA very far along in Latin America until the year 2005.

On that basis, let's start over again and think about what we are trying to do. To end concretely with a proposal, let's put less emphasis on trade agreements and more emphasis on free trade. There are lots of other ways the United States could approach this problem. The problem is not enough growth in the Western Hemisphere either for ourselves or for Latin America. We'd all like to have more growth. I don't think free trade agreements are the best way to get

there, given the political realities in the United States and our neigh-
boring countries. So instead we could propose various things.

One would be a temporary lowering of Himalayan tariffs that
we have in the United States down to a low flat level for Latin
America. A period of 5 years or 10 years would allow Latin America
to respond. We could unilaterally offer an expanded trade opportunity
and see how Latin America responds. If it responds in kind, if we
could get that momentum going, for example, with Brazil, this would
be very pro-growth for both countries. It would also lead to a pattern
where we could then turn to the Japanese and say 'hey look, you do
the same with us, show us something unilaterally and we'll look for
ways to respond." That would keep us from having to go through
these years of negotiations. I don't know if it would work, but I think
it gets us more directed toward the goal.

A second concept that we could work on is fully tariffying,
that means turning quotas into tariffs or auctioning off quotas. In the
western hemisphere, one of the most distortive things is the U.S.
practice of very intricate quotas that are blocking trade.

Another proposal: As presidents plan hemispheric summits
and get together to talk, one of the things that we should
ask—separately from free trade as a goal for the western hemisphere—is whether we aren't closer now to the point where we would
do better to aim for a goal of hemispheric balanced budgets. Couldn't
we get as much out of working with Latin countries to lock out
government fiscal mismanagement for a long time. This would be a
good alternative to embarking on this process that is going to lead to
another 10,000–20,000 pages of documents in order to bring people
into free trade agreements that may not really expand trade from what
it would otherwise have been.

Let's move beyond free trade agreements. I know that this is
not the spirit of the symposium, but there's so much other work in the
world, and so much was already accomplished on free trade through
free trade agreements. They worked some good in the past but now
the agenda should be something else. It is not possible to get another
free trade agreement with the political dynamic that we have. It is not
clear that more free trade agreements should be anywhere near the top

of the priority list that we would have if we were looking for growth in Latin America and the United States.

Next Steps in Expanding NAFTA and Building Hemispheric Economic Integration: The View from Canada and the U.S. (II)

Prospects for Hemispheric Integration

Let me try to offer you a substantially different perspective from the one you've just heard. What I'd like to do—in a very short period of time—is talk about hemispheric integration past, present, and future.

The first point to make is that hemispheric integration has been a longstanding process. To be sure, progress has been achieved in fits and starts, but it has been going on for a long time in North America and in South America.

In North America, regional integration dates back at least to the 1960s with the U.S.-Canada Auto Pact and the start of the maquiladora program. In Latin America there were numerous integration efforts; most initially failed in the 1950s and 1960s due to competing import substitution strategies of the member countries. Basically, those integration efforts failed because the participants were trying to take advantage of each other rather than working with each other. But since the mid 1980s, there has been an economic revolution in Latin America; almost all countries have adopted market-oriented policies with a strong export orientation that has led

Jeffrey J. Schott, senior fellow at the Institute for International Economics, is also a Visiting Lecturer at Princeton University.

to a revival of economic growth throughout Latin America. This has been done both individually and in the context of subregional economic integration efforts in the Mercosur, the Andean group, the Central American Common Market, and in the Caribbean.

The integration of North America and the integration in Latin America were linked in 1990 by the Enterprise of the Americas Initiative, which was launched just barely two weeks after the announcement of prospective U.S.-Mexico free trade talks. Perhaps not surprisingly, the Enterprise for the Americas Initiative, which is really at the heart of what is going to be discussed in Miami this weekend, received a very warm reception throughout Latin America, for two reasons.

Latin American countries were concerned in 1990 about continued good access to the U.S. market because of a perceived growth in U.S. protectionism and fear about the possible failure of the Uruguay Round, which was then going through difficult times. But, even more importantly, the warm reception in Latin America to the Enterprise of the Americas Initiative was due to the fact that the EAI reinforced the domestic economic reforms that those countries were undertaking. It provided some international encouragement and the possibility that they would be able to lock in their reforms to prevent policy reversals in subsequent administrations.

What is really driving the integration process in the Western Hemisphere are the domestic economic reforms being pursued throughout the region. These reforms encompass both unilateral trade liberalization, trade liberalization within the subregional groups, privatization of state owned enterprises, deregulation and above all macroeconomic reforms. The successful implementation of these policies is a prerequisite for hemispheric integration, without which developing countries will be unlikely to be able to assume, much less sustain, reciprocal free trade commitments and obligations with industrial countries.

In that regard, there is no example in the world of a developing country being able to go to free trade with industrial countries—except Mexico. And Mexico went through seven years of very difficult unilateral economic reform to put itself in a position where it could undertake those types of obligations. I think that's the most important lesson one can learn about economic integration in the hemisphere, and that is what is driving the process today.

Now, the Miami Summit is designed to reinforce those existing integration efforts and pave the way for closer trade investment ties throughout the hemisphere. We've had a long discussion of the Miami Summit this morning, so I won't repeat those issues except to note one additional point. When one refers to Western Hemisphere economic integration, one is really talking about integrating with the U.S., because the United States accounts for about 75 percent of the gross domestic product of the Western Hemisphere. So, you can talk about the importance of Mercosur, you can talk about the other subregional arrangements in Latin America, but the market of the Western Hemisphere is still predominately the U.S. market. That's why the NAFTA expansion model is essentially the one that is going to prevail over time, even if there is a more eclectic approach to getting there, as I'll discuss in a moment. But certainly the NAFTA establishes many important precedents for the future evolution of free trade arrangements in the Western Hemisphere.

This said, let me temper this optimistic assessment by noting that there are a number of constraints that face the rapid integration of economies in the Western Hemisphere.

First and foremost is the point that most countries, with the exception of Chile, are not yet ready to undertake reciprocal free trade rights and obligations. They haven't done their homework. Many have made significant progress in the last decade but they are not quite there. If their economic reforms are sustained, I wouldn't be surprised if a number of countries were able to undertake the type of obligations that Mexico has undertaken by the end of this decade. So I'm much more optimistic than David Malpass that there is scope for going further. But again, it's the domestic progress that will be the leading indicator of how far and how fast governments can work with one another to move forward to free trade.

The second constraint is one that has been mentioned often today, U.S. fast-track authority. I strongly disagree with David. It is not dead. However, there is a chasm between the Democrats and the Republicans over the terms of the renewal of fast track, especially with regard to the labor and environmental issues. I wish Senator

Lugar, who is quite knowledgeable and imaginative on these issues, would have addressed how to build the bridge between the two camps—I believe such a bridge is possible, if for no other reason than that Congress does not want to take responsibility for directing U.S. trade policy. Congress wants to have a hand on the rudder but it doesn't want to be the body responsible for the conduct of trade policy. And without fast track there won't be negotiations because there will be 535 hands trying to push that rudder and we'll end up just going around in circles. I believe fast track is the only pragmatic way that the Congress can allow the executive to conduct trade policy, and then bring it back for the traditional Congressional oversight and acceptance.

The third constraint is this: The NAFTA needs to be revised if it is to be expanded. Moreover, the revisions will be needed in sensitive areas such as the rules of origin, the dispute settlement provisions, and the administrative provisions. This isn't going to be an easy task for the United States, much less for the other countries of the region.

Take, for example, the problem of changing the rules of origin. The NAFTA rules have been aptly called 'tools of discrimination" that were drafted to protect particular industries. Increasing the number of NAFTA member countries expands the range of the territory that qualifies as regional content. It therefore means that the protectiveness of those rules will be diluted, and that will raise concerns. So the suggestions that David made to implement reforms incrementally on a unilateral, or even a negotiated basis, run right into this protectionist windmill.

Revisions to the dispute settlement provisions may be equally troublesome. The NAFTA contains an innovative process that deals with disputes regarding the use of anti-dumping and countervailing duties. Mexico was accorded the right to challenge final AD and CVD decisions in the United States and Canada, if it overhauled its own laws and regulations to match those of its neighbors. The U.S. and the Canadian negotiators thought they were doing a great thing by requiring Mexico to adopt U.S. and Canadian norms. Instead they created a monster. Mexico now has a new division of the Commerce Ministry that is designed to process anti-dumping cases. And as good bureaucrats, they are going to work long and hard to make sure that their existence is justified. So Mexico is now in the business of imposing more and more anti-dumping duties, which have the effect of rolling back some of the liberalization that was implemented unilaterally and in the context of NAFTA. U.S. and Canadian exporters are feeling the brunt of such actions. Do we really want other countries in Latin America to follow the Mexican example?

Finally, let me turn to the prospects of regional integration. The evolving integration of the hemisphere is not going to follow the NAFTA expansion model solely or the subregional integration efforts solely. It is not an either/or proposition, contrary to the view spelled out this morning by Congressman Hamilton. It's really going to be a much more eclectic approach. The NAFTA will expand, indeed Chile is going to start that process next week, and subregional economic pacts are going to continue to expand. Moreover, countries will become more and more promiscuous and negotiate trade pacts with multiple partners. For example, Chile is going to be negotiating with the NAFTA at the same time that they're negotiating with the Mercosur on a free trade pact. Such cross cutting pacts could lead to the problem that Jules Katz noted earlier, to potentially conflicting rules and regulations.

To be sure, countries are sensitive to this problem. Mexico has attempted in their recent free trade agreements with Costa Rica, Colombia, and Venezuela to be as compatible as possible with the NAFTA, so that those pacts can eventually be subsumed in a broader integration pact. Mercosur will pose more of a problem in this regard because of the nature of the Customs Union as opposed to a free trade agreement, and because of some internal inconsistencies regarding the coverage of capital goods.

Allow me a final word, if I may, on the integration process. I think David is right that the Summit is likely to come out with an end date for the negotiation of a free trade agreement in the hemisphere by the year 2005. There are risks and benefits in setting a date. On the one hand, the experience of past trade negotiations demonstrates that once one sets a target, business usually runs far ahead of the government negotiators. It happened in Europe with the announcement of the internal market reforms under the 1992 process. It happened in the

U.S.-Canada Free Trade Agreement. It happened in the NAFTA, where investors flooded into Mexico long before the negotiations were complete. So setting a target completion date can be a signal to investors that accelerates the pace of integration.

On the other hand, one can't dismiss the possibility that there will be foot draggers that use the target date as an excuse for slowing down the process of working within regional groups. Indeed, one of the reasons why you are likely to see an eclectic approach to integration—both NAFTA expansion and subregional expansion—is that some of the subregional groups are going to slow down because of foot draggers. Brazil may well slow down the Mercosur process—that is why countries that are talking to Brazil are also going to want to talk to the NAFTA countries and perhaps with others. To be sure, recent events in Brazil have been favorable, but Brazilian policymakers have a long way to go to restore confidence that their economic reforms will be sustained.

Overall I'm very optimistic about the prospects for Western Hemisphere economic integration, but I don't think it's going to be a neat process like Gary Hufbauer and I proposed in our book. I think it's going to be one where governments determine the success of the integration process more through their domestic economic reforms than through trade negotiations. If they get those reforms right, businesses will be five years ahead of them in achieving the goal of hemispheric free trade.

Next Steps in Expanding NAFTA and Building Hemispheric Economic Integration: The View from Canada and the U.S. (II)

RONALD J. WONNACOTT

Liberalizing Trade in the Americas: Are We Still on the Right Track?

I'd like to address two broad questions. First, in liberalizing trade in the hemisphere, where do we want to go? And second, how do we get there; are we on the right track?

On the first issue of specifying our eventual target, I have been asked to address the question: Do we aim for a full hemispheric free trade agreement (through, for example, the expansion of NAFTA or some broad all-inclusive negotiation) or is there a case to be made for a policy that has attracted some support in the United States in the last year—namely, the U.S. alone signing a series of bilateral agreements with individual Latin American countries or groups, starting with Chile? Or does it matter?

As we are meeting here, we are hearing relatively reliable reports that, unless something goes wrong, the Miami Summit this weekend will resolve the issue of where we are going with the announcement of the target of a hemisphere-wide free trade agreement by 2005. While this vision is exceedingly important, it will, according to reports, leave a number of critical issues outstanding. For example,

Ronald J. Wonnacott is William G. Davis Professor of International Trade, University of Western Ontario what are the provisions that will govern our trade with countries outside the hemisphere? Moreover, the other question 'How we get there?' will still be far from fully answered. To what degree will an all-hemispheric negotiation be preceded by an expansion of NAFTA? There are reports that negotiations will be announced this weekend for expanding NAFTA to include Chile; will other countries or groups also be included prior to an overall negotiation to bring the entire hemisphere together? Should guidelines be established to prevent countries or groups such as Mercosur from negotiating deals with outsiders like the EU? If such deals are done, what—if any—problems might they create?

In this paper I hope to throw light on some of these issues. Specifically, this paper will

1. confirm that the all-inclusive free trade agreement to be announced in Miami is not only where we will be going in the hemisphere; it is also where we should be going;

2. also confirm that if, en route to this objective, there is to be a free trade negotiation between North America and any individual country or group of countries in Latin America, it should be to include them—as Chile is now apparently to be included—in an expanding NAFTA; the alternative approach of the U.S. negotiating a bilateral free trade agreement with each of a series of Latin American countries—an option considered but rejected for Mexico in 1990 and for Chile in 1994—should continue to be rejected in the future;

3. show what is wrong with the maze of free trade areas in Latin America—deals that may have seemed reasonable enough considered in isolation, but when examined together make up a near chaotic trading pattern;

4. show why deals with outsiders (such as the proposed agreement between Mercosur and the EU) that, again, may seem reasonable enough when viewed in isolation, would raise profound problems for the hemisphere;

5. also provide a framework for examining the liberalization of East-West trade in Europe that is now taking place. But that's another story.

Where Are We Now?

Panel 1 of the Figure shows the 1989 Canada-U.S. free trade agreement (FTA), the big trigger to the process of hemisphere liberalization. Now, six years later, that FTA is a done deal, except of course for the part of the deal that is not yet done—namely, the reform of contingent protection, the black hole in the Canada-U.S. FTA that still remains in NAFTA.[1] By 1990, Mexico sought to liberalize its trade with the United States in much the same way, and U.S.-Mexican negotiations were about to begin. The question arose as to whether Canada should participate in transforming the Canada-U.S. bilateral into what, in the actual event, became the trilateral NAFTA agreement (panel 3); or whether Canada should stand aside, thus avoiding dragging the whole sensitive issue of trade liberalization back center stage into the political arena, and let the United States and Mexico negotiate a bilateral (panel 2). That would have created a system in which the United States would have become a hub with two bilateral spoke agreements: one with Canada, and another with Mexico. A major characteristic of such a system of overlapping free trade agreements would have been that Canadian-Mexican trade would not have been liberalized, whereas in the full FTA in panel 3 it was liberalized.

With Chile next on the agenda, essentially the same issue has arisen this year. Should NAFTA be expanded to include Chile (panel 4), or should the United States sign a spoke bilateral with Chile (panel 6)? If present reports hold up, this question will be answered this weekend with the announcement of negotiations for Chilean accession to NAFTA (panel 4). (At that point, of course, NAFTA would have to be called something else: The obvious name would be the Americas

---

[1]Unless specified more precisely, FTA will be used as a generic term (like CU in the past trade theory literature) to represent any FTA or CU agreement that provides for free trade among its members. In this paper, I will be talking about expectations rather than guarantees; and tariffs will refer to any barriers to trade.

FIGURE 1
Architecture of Hemispheric Trade Liberalization

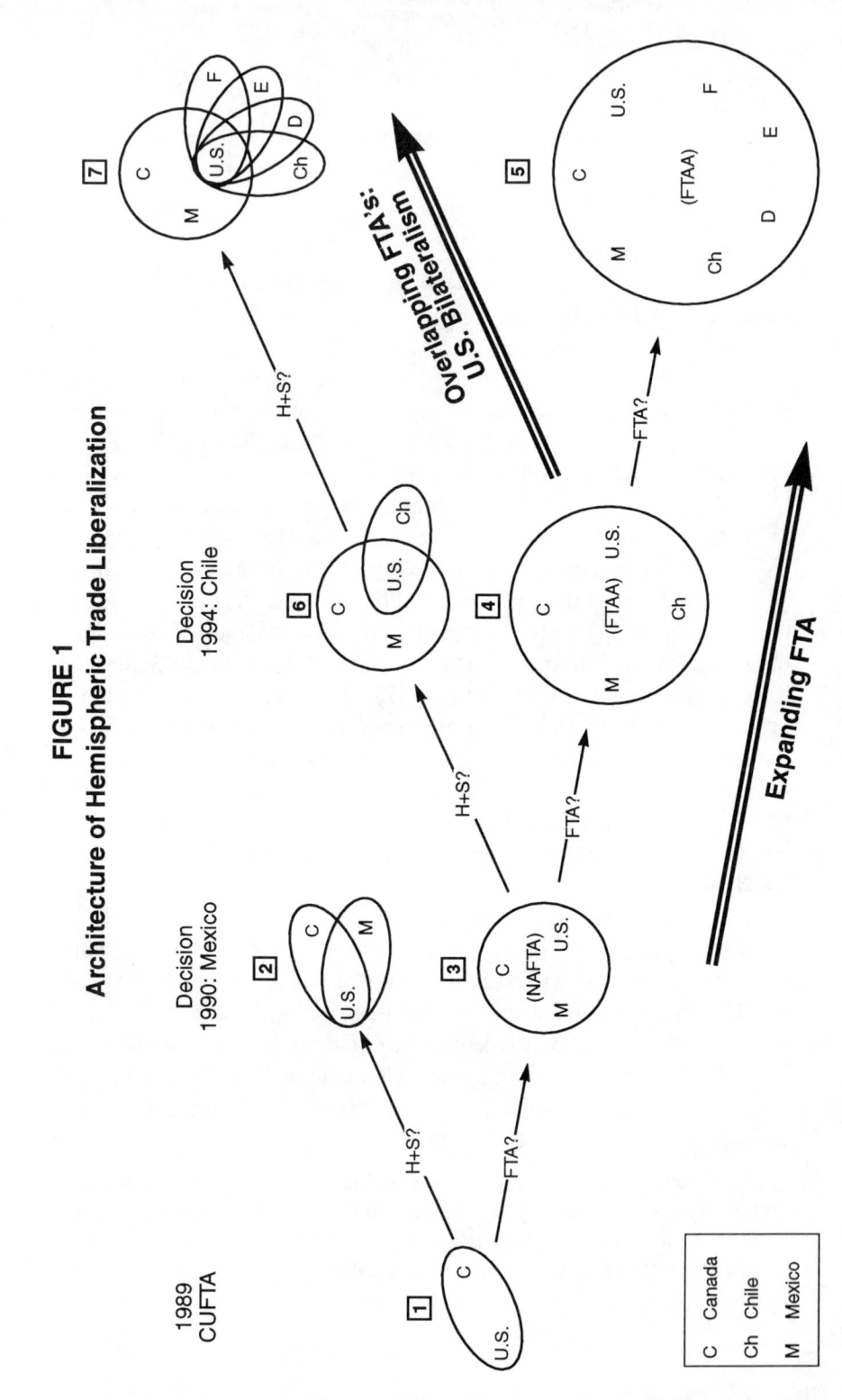

Free Trade Agreement [AFTA]. But since that acronym has already been taken by the Asean Free Trade Area, another possibility is the Free Trade Agreement of the Americas [FTAA], or simply 'FT double A."[2])

Even though a U.S. bilateral approach is now apparently being rejected in the Chilean case, there is no guarantee that the idea won't be proposed again for new candidate countries. It may have been thought in 1990 that, with the decision to go with NAFTA and thereby reject a U.S.-Mexican bilateral, the whole U.S. bilateral approach was dead. But not so, since this year there has been a revival of that possibility in dealing with Chile—and the idea could be revived again.[3]

This brings us then to the question: Should we now permanently reject such a bilateral approach—i.e., an approach that could lead to the U.S.-centered hub-and-spoke hemisphere of bilaterals depicted in panel 7 (or, in a move to panel 4 and thence to the northeast, to an outcome the same as panel 7 except that Chile would not be a spoke)? How would this compare to the all-inclusive free trade area shown in panel 5?

Hub-and-Spoke System Compared to an Expanding Free Trade Agreement

A hub-and-spoke system (H&S) would create a smaller income pie in the hemisphere. As we shall eventually see, there are many reasons for this. But one is obvious: trade distortions left between the spokes will reduce the potential free trade gains from this system.[4] However, the United States would get a larger share of the

---

[2]With 'triple A' status being reserved for eventual multilateral success in the WTO?

[3]Although probably not for the next two years, since the Republican-dominated U.S. Congress elected last month is unlikely to be susceptible to pressure from the labor and environmental groups that have generated the bilateral proposal.

[4]For a brief summary of why one need not be concerned with the one phenomenon that could upset this straightforward conclusion—namely, more serious damage from trade diversion in an FTA than in an H&S—see Ronald J. Wonnacott, "Hemispheric Liberalization: An Expanding Free Trade

smaller income pie leaving the overall effect on the United States ambiguous. Why would the United States get a larger share (to keep it simple, in panel 2 vs. panel 3)? One reason is that the United States would get preference in Canada in competition with Mexico. (U.S. exports to Canada would be duty free, whereas Mexican exports to Canada would still face Canadian trade barriers.) A second reason is that the United States would similarly get preference in Mexico in competition with Canada. The resulting increase in the demand for its exports would provide it with an income advantage.[5] The United States would also get an investment advantage, since it would be the only location from which a firm could get duty-free access to the markets of all three participating countries.

However, it should be emphasized that this relative (but not absolute) advantage for the United States would be at the expense of spoke countries, which would 1) fail to get the benefits of free trade with each other; and 2) face damage to the conditions governing their spoke-spoke trade. The reason for this damage is that it would be more difficult for Canadian firms to export to Mexico because of the discrimination they would face there in competition with U.S. firms; and it would similarly be more difficult for Mexican firms to export to Canada.

Does the Adverse Effect on Spoke-Spoke Trade Matter?

Spoke-spoke (i.e., Canadian-Mexican) trade has been relatively small in the past (panel 2), representing only 1-2 percent of Canadian-U.S. trade. However it is growing rapidly; in this first year of the NAFTA, it is up 30 percent over last year. Although this does not yet give us an adequate fix on the potential for growth, Canadian-Mexican trade can no longer be dismissed in the way it could have been even a few years ago. The most significant reason however for liberalizing Canadian-Mexican trade in NAFTA (panel 3) rather than

---

Area or a Set of U.S. Bilaterals?" University of Western Ontario, Centre for the Study of International Economic Relations Working Paper 9402C, 1994, footnote 2.

[5]It would also get a cost (and hence income) advantage over Canada and Mexico because only U.S. firms would be able to acquire duty-free inputs from both spokes.

leaving it damaged in the H&S in panel 2 is not the growth in this trade, but the precedent this has set for future agreements; this started us moving to the Southeast in the Figure, rather than to the Northeast. (While Jules Katz mentioned that we may not have been in complete agreement on the importance of the H&S vs. FTA issue in the early negotiating days of NAFTA, on the importance of rejecting the H&S as a precedent, I understand that we are in complete agreement.)

An important reason why the NAFTA precedent has been so important is the large expected growth in Latin American economies that will eventually, in the FTAA, make them much larger traders with each other. Given this increased potential for trade within Latin America—and the feedback effects it will have in further increasing Latin American incomes—it is essential to establish a system that improves rather than damages the conditions governing this trade.

Growth Potential in Latin America

Why is there such large growth potential in Latin America? Partly, as in Southeast Asia, it will be the expected payoff from domestic reforms. However, for two reasons Latin American growth may not only match, but may possibly even exceed, the recent high rates in Southeast Asia. First, Latin American countries, unlike those in Southeast Asia, will have free access to the U.S. market, which is so critical for growth in any developing country. Second, in trading with the United States, Latin American countries face no Pacific Ocean that swallows up some of the gains from U.S.-Southeast Asian trade. Clearly this second advantage is greater for Mexico than for Latin American countries farther to the south.

One might ask what the growth potential might be, for example, in a Latin American country like Mexico, where productivity and income are now, at best, somewhere in the range of 20-25 percent of U.S. levels. Multinational corporations report that productivity in Mexico on the shop floor can be much higher than the Mexican average when Mexican labor is combined with state-of-the-art production techniques and the required capital equipment. Indeed, in some cases, Mexican productivity has approached or equaled that in the United States. True, a nation's productivity depends on other factors such as its transportation and telecommunications infrastructure, and in the Mexican case, this may take considerable time to upgrade. Nonetheless if, in the next decade or so, the present gap in productivity—and hence eventually income—between Mexico and the United States were to be closed by just one third, Mexican productivity and income would more than double. The possibility then is that Canada and the United States, instead of being isolated as wealthy countries in a relatively poor hemisphere, will instead in the next decade or so be surrounded in the hemisphere by little—or not so little—tigers. In this kind of a world, trade among them is critical as a determinant of how fast they will grow. And the greater the trade and prosperity in Latin America in a hemispheric FTA (versus an H&S) the more important the effect on U.S. and Canadian export potential.

Other Problems with a Hub-and-Spoke System

Other special costs in an H&S will make spokes more strongly prefer an FTA and will make it more likely that the United States will, on balance, also judge an FTA superior.

1. Some trade in panel 7 between Latin American countries, say D and F, may be rerouted via the duty-free U.S. hub; but some will not. The question of sorting out the least-cost routing in an H&S will lead to a waste of real resources—firms hiring accountants, lawyers and economists—to calculate the best routing throughout this maze. Moreover, when rerouting does occur there is a waste in terms of excess transport costs and other costs. Note that these are above and beyond the efficiency losses described in the section above that would occur even in a world without transportation costs.

2. As an H&S develops, questions will arise like Which country will be next? and What will the provisions be? The result will be rent-seeking waste—the hiring of lawyers, lobbyists and others to attempt to affect the timing and terms of the bilateral agreements. Such rent-seeking competition may or may not be beneficial for the firms that engage in it, but it is a waste from the social point of view.

3. The above costs will be incurred even if all the bilateral agreements in an H&S are consistent (negotiations, so to speak, by word processor, with global replacement of names, leaving conditions identical). But they almost certainly won't be consistent since, in any bilateral, each of the two participating countries will want to tailor the agreement to its special needs. The result of inconsistent bilaterals will be an increase in all the problems above and the overall

inefficiency of the system. Moreover, inconsistent bilaterals create the risk that existing spokes will be sideswiped by a new spoke negotiating a better deal from the United States. In this case the existing spokes would face discrimination in the U.S. market, in addition, of course, to the discrimination they can't avoid in other spoke markets.

Conclusion: Towards a Hemispheric Free Trade Area

The Figure doesn't attempt to show the near-chaos of free trade agreements that already exist in Latin America (some that overlap, some that do not). Many of these agreements create little H&S systems centered, for example, on Mexico. In other cases, there are free trade agreements or customs unions that operate on their own. These agreements vary widely in terms of their provisions and the depth—or lack of it—of their liberalization. In such a complex trading regime, many exporters are simply giving up and paying MFN tariffs, in which case the gains from free trade are being lost.

To get some idea of how important this issue is, consider one possible system in which Mexico would become a hub. (It's already a hub in several smaller systems). The proposed Latin American free trade area would make Mexico a hub with a U.S.-Canadian spoke, and another spoke made up of all the rest of Latin America. In this system the spoke-spoke trade that would be damaged would be a substantial part of the trade in the hemisphere.

Whereas FTAA would enfold and eliminate all these free trade agreements, an H&S would, in the process of possibly reducing some of the chaos, add to it by injecting new elements of trade discrimination into the system.

Why does the United States not object to this development of overlapping FTAs in Latin America, or even to simpler, non-overlapping developments such as Mercosur in which it also faces discrimination? It beats me. Is it possible that it is inattention to what's going on, or even the view that any free trade agreement is good, whether or not you're in it, and whether or not it's part of a very complex and discriminatory trading system? I have a friend who doesn't put it this directly but often talks as though he's never met a free trade area that he hasn't fallen in love with. The U.S. administration used to strongly object to the extension of the European Community into the Mediterranean; now it doesn't seem even to object to similar developments on its own doorstep, such as the current tentative proposal for an EU-Mercosur agreement.

The other reason for getting it right now is the difficulty of reversing later policy we make today. There are a number of reasons why, once an H&S is established, it may be difficult to transform it into a corresponding FTA. This is true even in the simple case in panel 2 where a Canada-Mexico bilateral would apparently transform that system into panel 3. One reason it would not is that it would leave trade among the three countries subject to more demanding rules of origin. Secondly, there may not be the political will or the window of negotiating opportunity to get such a spoke-spoke negotiation. Third, if the system is comprised of many U.S.-centered spoke agreements (panel 7) the number of required bilateral agreements necessary to transform this into the FTAA in panel 5 multiplies rapidly. Another roadblock in such a transformation may be investment hysteresis: once an inefficient pattern of investment is established (with too little investment in the spokes, and in the system as a whole), it will continue in sectors with economies of scale and/or agglomeration influences where industry tends to stay where it is already located. As a consequence, investment may be mired in an inefficient H&S pattern, even if the trading system were to be transformed into an FTA by a broad negotiation including all spokes and the hub (essentially the only realistic way of accomplishing this FTA transformation once there is more than two spokes).

The conclusion that an expanding FTA is the appropriate route to take is not in dispute. I know of no trade theorist who disagrees with this conclusion. (In fact, one of the most prominent U.S. trade analysts, in addressing this issue, has put it succinctly: "Of course, that's the way we want to go.")

An H&S would be a bad deal even for the United States. Whereas a free trade agreement provides a vision of liberalized trade throughout the hemisphere with all countries trading equally, a U.S.-centered H&S would be viewed as a system in which, compared to an FTA, the United States would be perceived as increasing its already dominant position in the hemisphere by benefiting at the expense of its neighbors, which are (Canada excepted) far poorer—when in fact, because of the wastes and the consequent smaller overall income pie, the United States could not expect, on balance, to benefit at all.

An H&S would be an even worse deal for the spokes, not only because of the overall discriminatory architecture of the system, which would leave them with a smaller share of a smaller income pie, but also because the specific provisions any spoke would get in its bilateral agreement with the United States would likely be worse. An example is provided by Chile: If it were to try to negotiate a bilateral with the United States, it would almost certainly get less favorable access to the U.S. market than it would under NAFTA accession, since those U.S. domestic interests that would have successfully got the negotiations bilateralized have also been pressing for a strengthening of new U.S. trade remedies.

Provisions of FTAA: How Should They Be Modified As We Proceed?

1. A number of analysts have suggested making rules of origin less demanding. I'd go further and eliminate them entirely. They have become too expensive to comply with; they protect member countries against outsiders; and they also protect the large-market country against its partners, generating unnecessary conflicts among them.[6] The question is how do we eliminate rules of origin since this requires having a common external tariff? The answer lies in the precedent set in NAFTA in the computer industry—a precedent negotiated by two of the speakers at this conference, Jules Katz and John Weekes. In this industry, we have the right sort of a customs union, with a common but lower tariff (often zero) that can be

---

[6]To illustrate this less obvious effect in the case of NAFTA, note that, if a Japanese firm wishing to sell in the large U.S. market locates there, it does not have to satisfy any rule of origin since it will not be selling its product across any internal NAFTA border. But if it locates instead in Canada or Mexico, it must sell across the border into the United States and thus must satisfy a rule of origin. The stiffer the rule of origin, the greater this problem becomes for Japanese transplants in Canada or Mexico and the greater becomes their incentive to locate in the United States instead. Thus, more demanding rules of origin protect the United States—the country with the large market—from its "free trade" partners.

lowered further under special circumstances by individual members. In other words, in computers, NAFTA creates a customs union which avoids all the old "fortress CU" problems of increased common external barriers that can't be brought down without collective agreement.

2. No FTAA member should sign a bilateral agreement with an outsider. This is not an unreasonable requirement; it involves only accepting the simple discipline of a CU. Its common external tariff prevents any member from bilaterally negotiating any tariff reduction with any outsider.)

3. Set FTAA's provisions to minimize the resistance to an eventual move to multilateral free trade, in two ways:

(a) Maximize the competition within FTAA to get costs down to a near-world standard so the final move to world free trade will not involve a major dislocation. Thus, for example, we should avoid managed trade that, by restricting competition within FTAA, would generate less cost reduction.

(b) Ensure that FTAA will be open regionalism, i.e., an agreement that is open to outside competition. Specifically, the objective should be to lower trade barriers against outsiders, thus reducing the margins of preference that firms will have to give up in the final move to multilateral free trade.

4. For Mercosur or any other union in Central or South America, a similar approach is recommended. Reduce the resistance to an eventual move to a hemispheric free trade area (and multilateral free trade beyond). Again, the same guidelines should apply: Maximize competition within the union, and keep it open to outside competition. If such guidelines are followed, then there is great potential for such an agreement as a competitive workup to a hemisphere-wide FTA. On the other hand, the more any such agreement includes elements of managed trade, and the more barriers it leaves in place (or raises) against outside countries, the more damaging this type of agreement may be, since it would entrench discrimination in each of its member countries against all outsiders, in particular, against members of other FTAs in the hemisphere; thus the more difficult it

will make the task of eventually putting these agreements together by 2005.

In short, what we need is, first, a new statement of the vision of a full hemispheric free trade area of the Americas; second, a confirmation that Chile's accession to NAFTA will be negotiated in 1995, and, third, the assurance that the alternative H&S approach is rejected. Reports indicate that we will be getting the first two of these three out of Miami, which isn't bad at all—especially since the third may be implied. Thus we are still on the right track.

The reason that the vision, backed up by a concrete move with Chile, is important is not only because these offer substantial economic benefits, but also because they would help to preempt damaging developments that are otherwise more likely to occur, such as an agreement between Mercosur and the EU. Indeed we should go beyond this to express our strong opposition to both Mercosur and the EU to such a development, not only because it would immediately extend EU preferences into the Americas, leaving us all facing discrimination in Mercosur markets in competition with the EU; but also because, if we succeed in eventually constructing a hemispheric free trade area, a Mercosur hub would be created, with two enormous spokes: the rest of the Western hemisphere, and the EU. The spoke-spoke trade that would be damaged would be trade between the Western hemisphere (excluding Mercosur) and the European Union. This prospect should now—like the proverbial sight of the gallows—concentrate the mind, especially of anyone engaged in the formulation of trade policy.

Next Steps in Expanding NAFTA and Building Hemispheric Economic Integration: The View from Latin America (I)

Toward a Free Trade Zone from Alaska to Tierra del Fuego

Ladies and Gentlemen, I would like to thank the Fraser Institute and Hudson Institute for the opportunity to participate in this conference. This is a good opportunity to exchange points of view and to let you know what our expectations are.

During this decade, the international economic scene, and in particular the trade sector, demonstrated signs of profound change, including:

1. the tendency to form regional trade blocs, such as the European Union and the one formed by the U.S., Canada and Mexico;

2. the conclusion of the Uruguay Round of GATT and the approval of the agreement by the signatory countries.

3. and finally, the reduction of the foreign debt of developing countries, which at the same time implemented and strengthened structural reforms of great magnitude. This is the case of countries such as Argentina, which is en-

José María Ibarbia is a National Deputy, Republic of Argentina

deavoring to reverse its experience of the decade of the '80s.

Argentina's Point of View

Argentina has decided to modify its development strategy, opting for a market economy in the domestic arena, and in the international relations arena, for an alignment with the more developed western democracies, in particular with the United States.

The changes in economic policy undertaken by Argentina to facilitate re-entry into the international markets are the privatization of public companies (telephones, airlines, railroads, electrical power plants, etc.); deregulation of the economy; trade liberalization; and the re-orientation of the state toward the optimum administration of "public funds." All of these policies contribute to an increase in the efficiency of the economy, an improvement in the competitiveness of our producers, and the creation of a favorable climate for investors.

The policy most directly linked to international integration is the reform of foreign trade policy through liberalized treatment of foreign investment, establishing equal treatment for national and foreign capital.

Mercosur

Sub-regional integration is one of the key tools for enlarging the role of Argentina in the international economy. This is one of the fundamentals that brought about the signing of the Mercosur Treaty with Uruguay, Paraguay and Brazil. Mercosur has been defined by Argentina as one of the legs of the "spider strategy," referring to the need for multiple points of support for moving in many directions at once, which the process of integration with the rest of the world economy requires.

According to this vision, economic integration is conceived as the means by which Argentina and its partners will be able to improve the welfare of their citizens, while bringing their economies up to international standards of competitiveness. Different interests have led Argentina and Brazil to formalize the process of regional integration. In the case of Brazil, long term strategic supply is one of the main concerns; in Argentina's case, market expansion and economies of scale that brings are the expected results. At the same time, and for both participants, Mercosur is the ideal instrument to gain entry to the Enterprise of the Americas Initiative.[1]

Mercosur has meant an unexpected advance in the process of the integration of Latin America. The process had been initiated a few years before, notably on November 28, 1988, when the Treaty of Integration, Cooperation and Development between the Republic of Argentina and the Federal Republic of Brazil was signed. This treaty had as a goal, 'the removal of all obstacles, both tariffs and lack of tariffs, to the trade of goods and services." The process of integration between both countries was to conclude with the creation of a free trade zone within 10 years.

The Treaty of Asuncion—by which Mercosur was created—establishes in its first article the obligation among the signatory countries to structure a Common Market by December 31, 1994. The implications of such a Common Market are:

- The free movement of goods, services and production factors;

- The elimination of custom tariffs and quasi-tariff restrictions;

- The establishment of a common external tariff and the adoption of a common trade policy in relation to third countries, and the coordination of positions taken in regional and international economic forums;

- The coordination of sectoral and macroeconomic policies among the members;

- The agreement to harmonize national laws.

Even though this first article mentions the requirements for the functioning of the Common Market, it does not establish that they must all be completely developed by December 31, 1994. Instead it

---

[1]On June 19, 1991, Mercosur signed an agreement with the U.S. known as "Four Plus One," explicitly recognizing its presence at the international level. The agreement stipulates, among other things, that once Mercosur is structured, negotiations will continue between the U.S. and Mercosur, instead of bilaterally with the South American member states.)

establishes the obligation of the members to go ahead with the design of policies vital for the functioning of the Common Market.

Mercosur covers an area of almost 12 million square kilometers—five times larger than that of the European Union. It has a total population of 190 million people and a total gross product of close to $700 billion.

The process of integration has allowed a substantial increase of regional trade. Nevertheless, there are still questions about the future rate of integration. The inability to decrease the irregularities between the two major countries, specifically the current delays in the matter of coordination and reconciliation of macroeconomic policies, could make progress difficult.

In view of this reality, it is very important to distinguish clearly between long-term and short-term objectives. Providing businesses in the four countries with access to an expanded market is the central goal of the process of integration. This intermediate step will be an ideal way for them to improve their competitiveness in anticipation of a large and reciprocal open market with the rest of the world.

The evolution of Argentina's trade with the Mercosur members over the last six years has been significant. In 1988, the total volume of our trade with Mercosur was $2.045 billion, and Argentina had a trade deficit of $295 million (due to a deficit with Brazil). In 1993, the total volume of trade had almost quadrupled to $7.874 billion with Argentina running an overall deficit of $552 million ($779 million with Brazil).

In the intervening period, Argentina's volume of trade with all three countries increased, and Argentina enjoyed trade surpluses.

In 1993, the total volume of trade with the Mercosur countries increased by 29 percent over the previous year, with an increase of 57 percent in exports to the other three countries and a 12 percent increase in imports. It should be pointed out that exports to Brazil increased last year by 67 percent, with an 82.5 percent increase in the export of manufactured industrial goods. This increase is due specifically to the export of auto parts and finished vehicles, chemical products and petrochemicals, electric machinery and appliances, metal products, shoes, textiles and ready-to-wear clothing.

On Table 1 and Chart 1, you can see the summary of Argentina's trade evolution with Mercosur. In Charts 2 and 3, you can see the composition of Argentinian exports and imports, separated by economic impact, during the '92-93 period.

We have heard many times that the content of Argentinian exports to Mercosur, and specifically to Brazil, is based on products of low value-added. Nevertheless, if you analyze the values shown on Charts 2 and 3, you can see that while manufactures represent 28 percent of Argentinian exports to all countries, exports of manufactured goods to Brazil make up 39 percent of total exports to that country. (For the rest of the Mercosur countries, the percentage was 42.8.)

In Tables 2 and 3 are the data related to the origin and destination, by principal areas and countries, of the imports and exports of Argentina classified by economic type. We can see that in 1993, exports to Mercosur and Brazil represent 28 percent and 21 percent respectively of total exports.

It is important to emphasize the crucial role that exports to Mercosur have had on the overall growth of Argentina's exports. As you can see, from 1988 to 1993, total exports increased at an average annual rate of 7.5 percent, while Mercosur exports increased by an average yearly rate of 33.1 percent. This shows the impact that the integration with Mercosur has had on general Argentinian exports. At the same time, if you analyze imports over the same period, there is no substantial difference in the increase of imports from a specific point of origin.

Though the process of integration between Argentina and Brazil is taking place in the arena of trade liberalization by both countries, the process of automatic tariff reduction has also had a favorable impact on the level of trade between the two countries.

This was to be expected with the creation of a common market; some of the goods once produced locally are now imported from the new members, since the customs barriers within that market are eliminated. This shift in production from the local producer—at higher cost—to the foreign producer—at lower cost—is known as 'trade creation.' In the same fashion, there is increased consumption, since consumers now have access to similar goods at lower cost.

On the other hand, the creation of this common market means that some products that were previously imported from elsewhere in the world are now imported from the members due to the new tariff situation. There is clearly a displacement of these foreign products by those produced by members at a higher cost. This 'trade diversion' also effects the consumer, since now he must spend more to get similar goods which have artificially become more expensive due to tariffs. In other words, with the creation of a common market, the allocation of economic resources and the welfare of the participant countries can improve or deteriorate, depending basically on the common foreign tariff set for the product. In the case of Mercosur, trade creation is greater than the trade diversion phenomenon seen in chemical products, machinery and transportation equipment.

The intra-industrial trade that was already present before the Argentina/Brazil agreement was intensified by the process of tariff reduction allowing the generation of economies of scale derived from greater specialization and optimization at a higher level of production. This phenomenon can be seen in many industrial sectors depending on the intensity of changes in production.

The Common External Tariff in Mercosur

Because of the inexorability of the biannual increases of the Mercosur preference, together with the reduction of the 'list of exceptions" laid out on December 31, 1993—which made increasing quantities of goods automatically subject to lower taxes—the question of the common external tariff was destined to get the attention of the negotiators and authorities of the four member countries of Mercosur during the current year.

The common external tariff is an indispensable condition in order for the Customs Union to commence on January 1, 1995 as the basis of the Common Market that the Asuncion Treaty intends to establish. Without this common external tariff, only a Free Trade Zone would be attainable as a consequence of the conclusion and execution of the automatic and linear tariff tax reductions and the elimination of the exceptions. (There would remain only those corresponding to the year 1995 which were granted to Paraguay and Uruguay, as relatively less developed countries.)

The Asuncion Treaty established that the common external tariff, which was to be set in 1994, would not, as a general principle, discriminate in favor of particular sectors. It was also decided that the common external tariff would be fixed between 0 percent and 20 percent, and that a higher rate of 35 percent would be allowed for a limited number of products, with the requirement that this be reduced over a period of six years, starting on January 1, 1995, to a level no greater than 20 percent.

In spite of these provisions, which aim at establishing a benchmark that will override the anxiety of the protectionist sectors of the member countries, the politico-institutional and macro-economic instability that Brazil went through—in addition to an initial situation during which a high average tariff and a dispersion of tariffs higher than the ones in Argentina prevailed—have meant that our country was not able to finalize a favorable agreement on the common external tariff.

It is very difficult to imagine that the privileges which have remained untouched for years in certain sectors of the Brazilian industry—such as computer science, capital goods and chemical products—are going to be eliminated or reduced in a reasonable amount of time. In the area of the common external tariff, the constitution of Mercosur could become converts into a deadly trap. Argentina may have to decide if it will bow to the Mercosur producers of goods that are priced higher than they should be.

It is becoming obvious that the opportunity for Argentina to open its economy to international competition lies less and less with Mercosur, at least as on the terms that it is now established. A possible solution is to create a Mercosur that operates as a free trade zone (a 'SAFTA') and not as a Common Market, under which the ghost of the common external tariff would disappear. This would allow our country to maintain control of its trade policy, a fundamental element in reaching the objective of open trade.

In a Free Trade Zone or a Free Trade Association, the member countries agree to abolish the tariffs and quantitative restrictions between themselves but, as in the case of the preferential agreements, they do not adopt a common external tariff with respect to the rest of the world. In a Customs Union, by contrast, the countries agree on the abolition of the commercial barriers between themselves, and furthermore, they decide on the application of a common external tariff for the goods the Union imports.

All things considered, if the Argentinian objective is to increase the international competitiveness of its businesses, a Free Trade Zone would give us a free hand to manage our trade policy with the goal of establishing the best long term commercial strategy: *integration with the world economy and not just with one part of it*. This approach would also make it easier to add other countries, such as Chile, which are fearful of a common external tariff that "removes protection" from its strong export sector. We are of the opinion that Mercosur should not be considered as an end in itself but as a first step toward the more complete integration of the country into a global economy. The incorporation of Mercosur with NAFTA is a step that could free us from the trap of the common external tariff as currently negotiated.

Tables and Charts

Table 1
Argentina: Trade with the Mercosur Countries
(millions of dollars)

	1988	1989	1990	1991	1992	1993
Exports to Brazil	608	1,124	1,423	1,489	1,671	2,791
Imports from Brazil	971	721	717	1,526	3,336	3,570
Balance	-363	403	706	-37	-1,668	-779
Total trade	1,579	1,845	2,140	3,015	5,010	6,361
Exports to Uruguay	187	208	263	311	384	513
Imports from Uruguay	131	99	116	234	351	571
Balance	56	109	147	77	32	-58
Total trade	318	307	379	545	735	1,083
Exports to Paraguay	80	96	147	178	272	358
Imports from Paraguay	68	49	41	43	65	73
Balance	12	47	106	135	207	285
Total trade	148	145	188	221	337	430
Exports to Mercosur	875	1,426	1,833	1,978	2,327	3,661
Imports from Mercosur	1,170	869	874	1,803	3,755	4,213
Balance	-295	559	959	175	-1,429	-552
Total trade	2,045	2,297	2,707	3,781	6,082	7,874

Source: INDEC

Chart 1
Argentina: Trade with the Mercosur Countries
(millions of dollars)

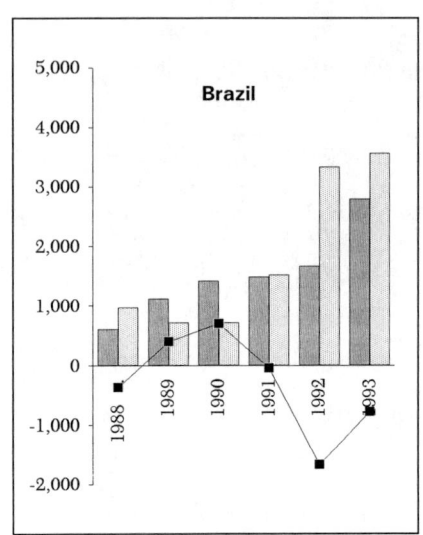

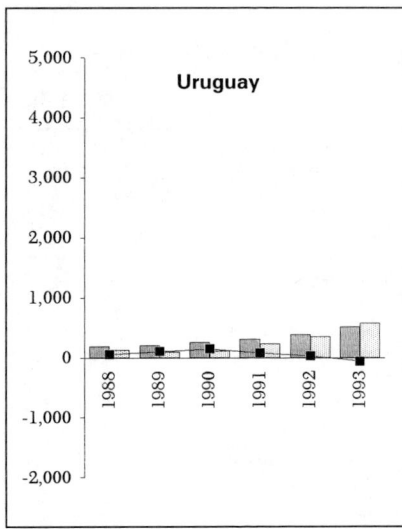

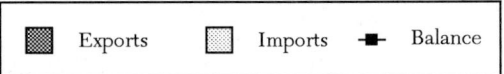

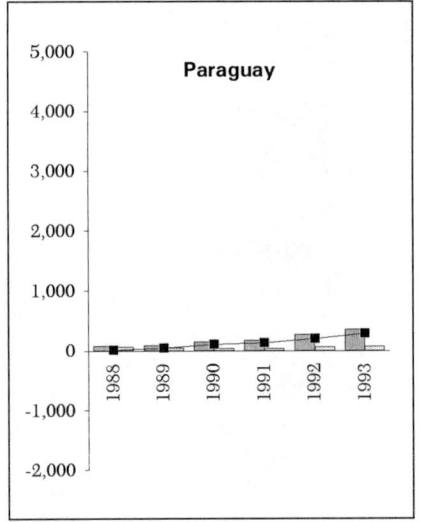

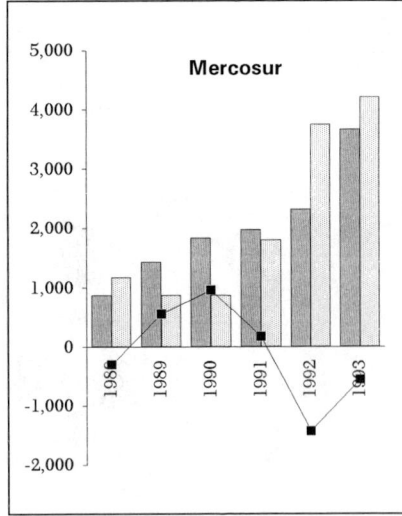

Chart 2
Argentina: Composition of Exports to Mercosur

1992

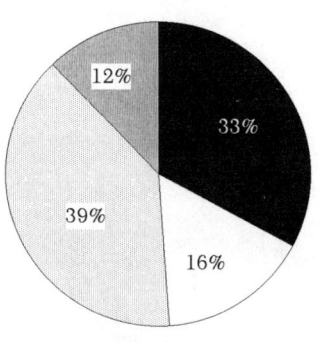

■ Raw materials □ Agricultural ▨ Manufactures ▨ Fuels

1993

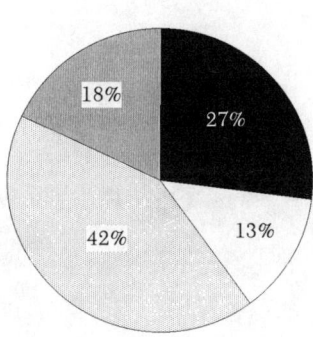

Chart 3
Argentina: Composition of Imports from Mercosur

1992

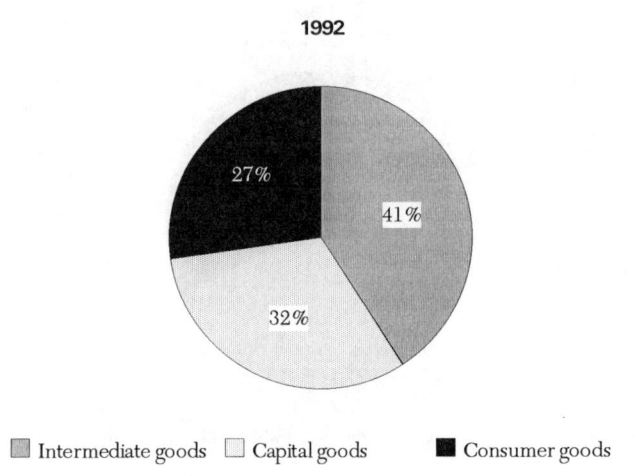

◫ Intermediate goods ▢ Capital goods   ■ Consumer goods

1993

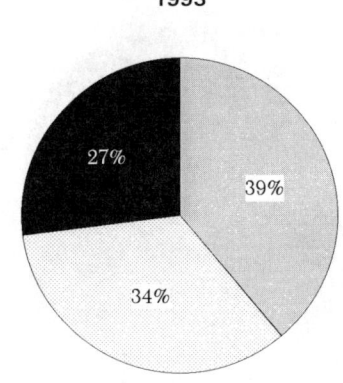

Table 2
Argentina: Exports by Sector and Destination
(millions of dollars)

	1988	1989	1990	1991	1992	1993[a]	Rate of change 93/92	Rate of change 93/88	Percent 1988	Percent 1993
Mercosur										
Total exports	875.2	1,428.0	1,832.7	1,977.1	2,326.9	3,661.1	57.3	33.1	100.0	100.0
Raw materials	227.2	371.6	582.4	622.4	772.2	909.4	17.8	32.0	26.0	24.8
Agricultural	131.0	305.8	365.3	402.3	360.0	511.9	42.2	31.3	15.0	14.0
Manufactures	477.8	674.5	766.6	797.3	906.1	1,567.1	73.0	26.8	54.6	42.8
Fuels	39.2	76.1	108.4	155.1	288.6	672.7	133.1	76.6	4.5	18.4
Brazil										
Total exports	607.9	1,124.0	1,422.7	1,488.5	1,671.3	2,790.5	67.0	35.6	100.0	100.0
Raw materials	210.6	346.3	560.3	591.9	711.2	865.5	21.7	32.7	34.6	31.0
Agricultural	93.7	258.6	305.8	335.1	242.3	343.3	41.7	29.7	15.4	12.3
Manufactures	299.4	499.7	550.7	533.1	596.4	1,088.2	82.5	29.4	49.3	39.0
Fuels	4.2	19.4	5.9	28.4	121.5	493.7	306.3	159.4	0.7	17.7
NAFTA										
Total exports	1,403.0	1,387.1	2,067.8	1,516.7	1,638.4	1,556.8	-5.0	2.1	100.0	100.0
Raw materials	103.3	106.1	184.2	140.2	167.0	160.5	-3.9	9.2	7.4	10.3
Agricultural	604.0	542.8	702.7	695.7	681.1	640.4	-6.0	1.2	43.1	41.1
Manufactures	622.3	574.8	537.3	443.5	444.3	617.0	38.9	-0.2	44.4	39,.6
Fuels	73.4	163.4	643.6	237.3	346.0	138.9	-59.9	13.6	5.2	8.9
United States										
Total exports	1,185.0	1,151.7	1,665.0	1,210.0	1,349.4	1,273.4	-5.6	1.4	100.0	100.0
Raw materials	82.3	85.2	79.7	67.8	103.6	88.2	-14.9	1.4	6.9	6.9
Agricultural	478.5	421.9	511.8	563.2	562.5	526.3	-6.4	1.9	40.4	41.3
Manufactures	552.0	489.7	434.0	344.3	340.4	522.4	53.5	-1.1	46.6	41.0
Fuels	72.2	154.9	639.5	234.7	342.9	136.5	-60.2	13.6	6.1	10.7
EC (EU)										
Total exports	2,726.4	2,500.5	3,743.6	3,956.2	3,819.4	3,650.2	-2.1	6.0	100.0	100.0
Raw materials	1,038.8	602.1	1,280.9	1,584.8	1,269.6	1,174.5	-8.1	2.5	38.1	32.2
Agricultural	1,300.1	1,388.1	1,733.3	1,878.5	1,966.3	1,918.3	-2.5	8.1	47.7	52.6
Manufactures	370.8	460.3	646.1	395.9	409.2	385.3	-6.2	0.8	13.6	10.6
Fuels	16.7	50.0	83.3	97.0	174.3	172.1	1.3	59.4	0.6	4.7
Total Exports	9,134.8	9,579.3	12,352.5	11,977.8	12,234.9	13,090.3	7.0	7.5	100.0	100.0
Raw materials	2,402.1	2,044.5	3,339.1	3,301.2	3,500.2	3,271.9	-6.5	6.4	26.3	25.0
Agricultural	3,943.0	4,005.7	4,663.9	4,927.4	4,829.4	4,928.8	2.1	4.6	43.2	37.7
Manufactures	2,632.8	3,185.9	3,364.3	2,983.5	2,823.4	3,665.5	29.8	6.8	28.8	28.0
Fuels	156.9	343.3	985.2	765.7	1,081.9	1,224.1	13.1	50.8	1.7	9.4

[a] Preliminary 1993 figures. The 93/88 rate of change is an average annual rate for the period.

Table 3
Argentina: Imports by Sector and Origin

	(millions of dollars)						Rate of change		Percent	
	1988	1989	1990	1991	1992	1993[b]	93/92	93/88	1988	1993
Mercosur (total)	1,169.8	869.0	875.2	1,804.4	3,754.7	4,213.6	12.2	29.2	100.0	100.0
Capital goods	92.6	71.5	76.5	183.6	445.5	571.5	28.3	43.9	7.9	13.6
Parts & accessories	146.2	110.5	141.4	318.5	754.4	913.1	21.0	44.2	12.5	21.7
Industrial supplies	760.6	611.9	566.7	934.6	1,502.3	1,510.4	0.5	14.7	65.0	35.8
Fuels	54.4	3.8	5.1	6.7	28.0	96.7	245.4	12.2	4.6	2.3
Consumer goods	102.1	62.1	68.0	260.9	619.3	720.2	16.3	47.8	8.7	17.1
Automotive	11.8	6.1	6.2	96.6	399.8	394.7	-1.3	101.8	1.0	9.4
Other	2.2	3.2	11.4	3.4	5.4	6.9	27.8	26.0	0.2	0.2
Brazil (total)	971.4	721.3	717.9	1,526.3	3,338.8	3,569.9	6.9	29.7	100.0	100.0
Capital goods	80.9	64.9	64.1	167.4	414.4	472.8	14.1	42.3	8.3	13.2
Parts & accessories	133.7	99.0	129.9	291.2	721.9	874.7	21.2	45.6	13.8	24.5
Industrial supplies	647.1	517.0	474.7	801.1	1,333.9	1,346.1	0.9	15.8	66.6	37.7
Fuels	50.0	0.6	0.6	5.1	23.4	89.4	282.1	12.3	5.2	2.5
Consumer goods	58.6	39.2	41.2	171.9	480.0	567.4	18.2	57.5	6.0	15.9
Automotive	0.0	0.0	0.1	87.3	360.7	214.0	-40.7	652.0	0.0	6.0
Other	0.9	0.7	7.3	2.4	4.4	5.5	25.0	43.6	0.1	0.2
U.S. (total)	908.2	880.5	861.5	1,845.2	3,226.3	3,858.6	19.6	33.6	100.0	100.0
Capital goods	210.4	226.9	179.9	477.9	1,149.1	1,616.2	40.6	50.3	23.2	41.9
Parts & accessories	179.0	145.5	143.8	240.7	394.1	369.6	-6.2	15.6	19.7	9.6
Industrial supplies	428.6	411.6	422.9	695.3	893.3	1,058.4	18.5	19.8	47.2	27.4
Fuels	41.4	49.7	39.8	47.2	56.2	66.1	17.6	9.8	4.6	1.7
Consumer goods	47.4	45.1	72.4	374.5	672.0	656.9	-2.2	69.2	5.2	17.0
Automotive	0.1	0.1	0.6	6.6	53.1	86.0	62.0	314.8	0.0	2.2
Other	1.4	1.7	2.2	3.0	8.6	5.4	-37.2	31.6	0.2	0.1
EC (EU) (total)	1,560.8	1,143.6	1,117.9	2,033.2	3,633.4	3,436.2	-5.4	17.1	100.0	100.0
Capital goods	405.2	293.1	248.1	476.1	954.0	919.3	-3.6	17.8	26.0	26.8
Parts & accessories	446.1	259.2	244.0	394.9	828.9	810.0	-2.3	12.7	28.6	23.6
Industrial supplies	632.4	522.7	536.9	838.0	1,143.2	1,062.9	-7.0	10.9	40.5	30.9
Fuels	27.6	20.4	7.9	23.7	34.8	22.8	-34.5	-3.8	1.8	0.7
Consumer goods	48.8	47.0	72.6	264.4	525.1	474.3	-9.7	57.6	3.1	13.8
Automotive	0.3	0.2	0.9	33.2	142.1	141.5	-0.4	234.1	0.0	4.1
Other	0.4	1.0	7.5	2.8	5.5	5.4	-2.5	71.9	0.0	0.2
Total	5,321.6	4,203.2	4,076.7	8,275.4	14,871.8	16,786.0	12.9	25.8	100.0	100.0
Capital goods	904.4	745.0	635.6	1,435.0	3,095.2	4,115.4	33.0	35.4	17.0	24.5
Parts & accessories	1,052.7	700.5	690.9	1,236.6	2,591.1	2,808.6	8.4	21.7	19.8	16.7
Industrial supplies	2,581.4	2,157.8	2,069.1	3,419.2	4,742.1	5,065.7	6.8	14.4	48.5	30.2
Fuels	494.1	365.5	315.9	452.0	415.8	386.3	-7.1	4.8	9.3	2.3
Consumer goods	272.0	220.8	330.3	1,514.2	3,204.7	3,526.7	10.0	66.9	5.1	21.0
Automotive	12.3	6.6	11.7	202.2	792.9	849.3	7.1	133.3	0.2	5.1
Other	4.6	7.1	23.1	16.1	29.9	34.0	13.7	49.2	0.1	0.2

[b] Preliminary 1993 figures. The 93/88 rate of change is an average annual rate for the period.

Next Steps in Expanding NAFTA and Building Hemispheric Economic Integration: The View from Latin America (II)

CRISTIÁN LARROULET

Introduction

In this paper I am going to examine the economic and commercial perspectives of Latin America after the NAFTA, or North American Free Trade Agreement—the U.S., Canada and Mexico free trade agreement which started operating this year.

It is clear to any informed analyst of the region, that in recent years Latin America has moved forward with widespread reforms that aim towards a greater liberalization of their economies.

Even though this occurred before the existence of NAFTA, I will argue that the North American Free Trade Agreement is—or should be—a very important instrument for advancing further towards free trade, free-market reform, greater economic growth, and eradication of extreme poverty in Latin America. On the other hand, I will maintain that if NAFTA should instead move towards a closed bloc, not extending southwards, it could cause undesirable effects, some of which I will examine here.

Cristián Larroulet is Executive Director of Instituto Libertad y Desarrollo (The Institute for Liberty and Development), and Dean of Micro and Macroeconomics, Economics Department, at the University for Development in Concepcion, Chile.

Economic Reforms in Latin America.

In the mid 1970s, when nearly all of the Latin American countries were following inward-looking, import substitution strategies, which began to be implemented after the Great Depression of the 1930s, Chile decided to swim against the tide and initiate a structural reform based on the free market and an open economy. After decades of socialist-populist policies, the economy was in a disastrous state; investment was low, the productive processes were nearly obsolete, there was little product differentiation, a high degree of market concentration, heavy state intervention in the economy, and a balance of payments crisis. Under such conditions, with tremendous market and price distortions, resource allocation was inefficient, and the potential for growth was limited.

It was under these inauspicious conditions that Chile's reforms began, and precisely for that reason, they had to first face the macroeconomic disequilibria and create the stability that was the precondition for the structural reforms undertaken later.

Along with the restoration and preservation of macroeconomic equilibrium, the main reforms focused on creating incentives for the growth of the private sector. This would be accomplished by reducing the size of the public sector—to create "breathing space" for private firms and individuals—and by creating the necessary conditions for growth. The reduction of the state was managed principally through privatization and a deep fiscal reform, including reductions in companies' taxes, thus favoring investment. The fiscal reform included a redefinition of the role of the state, leaving it with greatly reduced regulatory and financial powers.

These reforms also implied a fundamental rethinking of the role of the public sector, leaving behind the welfare state and focusing instead on regulating and creating markets rather than distorting them. This led to radical changes: privatization, price liberalization, elimination of quotas, deregulation of foreign investment, and reforms of the pension system, the educational system, health care, and others.

The trade policies, on the other hand, pursued various ends, among which were the generation of more jobs, the elimination of monopolies, an increase in consumption, and other initiatives which were expected to finally lead to economic development. Of these policies, I would like to stress the tariff and customs reform. Before this reform, international trade in Chile faced all sorts of tariff and non-tariff restrictions. There were restrictive, or at least very high tariffs, prohibitions to import and export certain goods, quotas, requirements of previous imports deposits and very high customs duties.

Other structural reforms that had a positive effect on the opening of the economy were the foreign investment legislation, which established a clear and stable framework for foreign businesses; the creation of a national export promotion agency, which acts as a sort of commercial representative providing information on the Chilean markets and its export products; the capital market reform, which, inter alia, eliminated interest rate and capital controls thus making the saving-investment intermediation easier; transport reform, which promoted competition in the shipping, road and airline transport industries; the ports reform, which eliminated a public monopoly and has resulted in highly efficient Chilean ports; and, last but not least, the labor reform, which has eliminated several regulations that distorted the labor market, and was a very important reform in terms of the comparative advantages that mean so much for a trade-oriented economy such as Chile's.

Throughout the 1970s, and into at least the first half of the 1980s, most Latin American countries persisted in inward-looking and statist policies. The results were disastrous, as they had been in Chile in the past, and Latin America found itself falling further and further behind other regions of the world, particularly Asia (see Figure 1).

The debt and development crisis of the 1980s, which led to the so called "lost decade," made a deep impression on Latin America's policy makers. The failure of the old paradigm, and the evidence that an import-substitution strategy was unable to deliver better growth and deal with the crisis of the period, gave rise to pressure for reform, and a reevaluation of the role of the state in economic life in Latin America, which was also noticed by politicians, voters and the population in general.

Even though, as we shall see later, there were great differences in the extent to which these policies were applied, virtually every country in the region undertook some type of economic reform and, over the course of a decade or so, many countries abandoned the

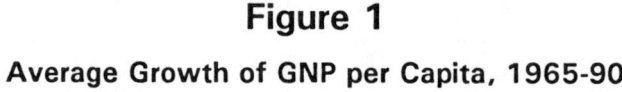

Figure 1

Average Growth of GNP per Capita, 1965-90

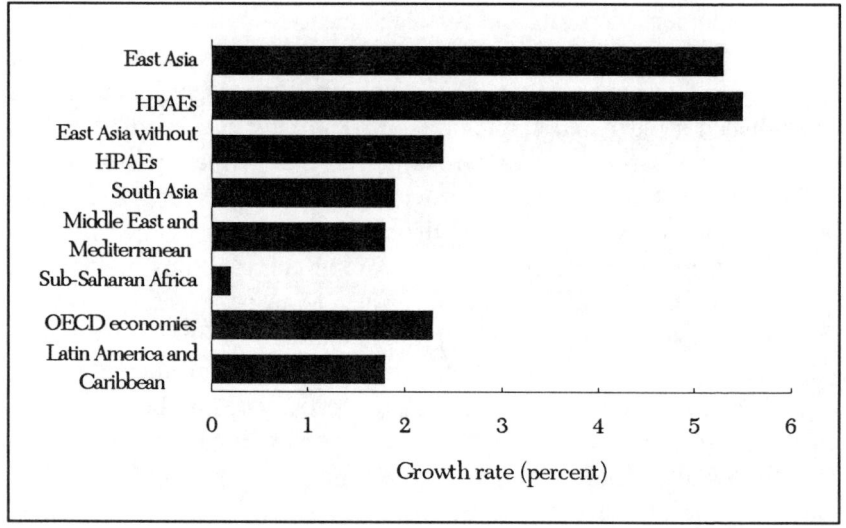

import-substitution policies of the past for macroeconomic reform combined with export-oriented, free-market policies.

Since the main cause of macroeconomic imbalances had been the huge explosion in fiscal deficits in many countries in the earlier '80s, these had to be addressed first. Accordingly, fiscal reforms were implemented in Bolivia, Peru, Mexico, Uruguay and elsewhere. As part of the fiscal discipline, these reforms also included tax reforms and privatization as a means to increase efficiency, reduce the government's fiscal burden and, additionally, create a positive environment for growth.

Privatization is, and has been in recent years, a significant phenomenon in Latin America. Indeed, with the exception of the formerly centralized economies of Eastern Europe and the ex-Soviet Union, nowhere else in the world has privatization been as significant as in Latin America (see Figures 2 and 3).

Of course, a policy is not sound simply because it is widespread. But the evidence tends to show that the privatizations have

Figure 2

Privatization in Latin America in Selected Countries

Country	Enterprises privatized	Main Sectors	GDP (percent)	Income (millions)
Argentina	84 [a]	Public services, petrochemical, petroleum, airlines	5.3 (1992)	$12,135
Brazil I [b]	38	Textiles, forest	0.2 (1990)	$824
Brazil II	22	Petrochemical, fertilizers, steel	1.4 (1992)	$6,648
Chile I [c]	325	Agricultural, other	7.0	$952
Chile II	207	Social Security, public services, health, financial, industrial	6.1	$1,349
Mexico [d]	930	Textiles, mining, petrochemical, drugs, banks, telecom., airlines, steel, automobiles	6.4 (1992)	$21,247
Peru	41	Mining, cement, public services, petroleum	10.8 (1993)	$2,622

Source: Lüders (1994)

---

[a] Includes 57 privatized state-owned enterprises and 27 concessions.
[b] Brazil I: 1979-1990. Brazil II: 1991-1993.
[c] Chile I: 1974-1979. Chile II: 1985-1990. In the case of Chile, percent of GDP revenues was computed for each year and added.
[d] Until the end of 1992, 930 state-owned enterprises were in the process of being privatized or liquidated.

Figure 3

Privatizations, 1988-1992: Total revenues per capita (U.S. dollars)

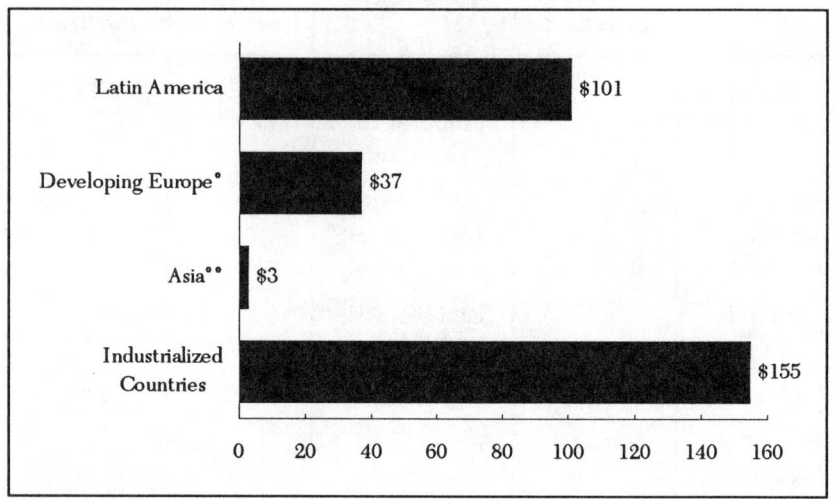

Source: World Bank

* Eastern Europe and Turkey
** Excluding Japan

been welfare-enhancing (see, for example, Galal et. al.), particularly in Chile. Lüders and Hachette (1992) show conclusively that Chile's privatizations did not diminish the resources of the state; that they had, if anything, a positive employment effect; that they contributed to the rapid development of a capital market; that they did not produce a significant improvement in efficiency, because the state owned enterprises were already being treated like private firms; and that they contributed to the overall success of the Chilean development model, because of their favorable impact on the growth of the private sector.

In short, the fiscal reform and the privatization process were crucial to creating a new business climate, in which greater fiscal discipline reduced the crowding out of the private sector in financial markets that had occurred due to higher interest rates and inflation (see Figures 4 and 5).

Figure 4

Real GDP Growth (percent)

	1985	1986	1987	1988	1989	1990	1991	1992	1993
Argentina	-5.1	5.2	2.7	-2.1	-5.2	-0.1	8.9	8.6	6.0
Bolivia	-1.0	-2.5	2.6	3.0	2.7	4.7	5.3	2.0	3.0
Brazil	7.9	7.6	3.6	-1.0	3.3	-4.4	0.9	-1.0	5.0
Colombia	3.8	6.9	5.6	4.2	3.5	4.0	1.9	3.6	5.2
Chile	3.5	5.6	6.6	7.3	9.9	3.3	7.3	11.0	6.3
Mexico	2.6	-3.8	1.9	1.1	-0.2	4.7	3.6	2.6	0.4
Peru	2.3	8.7	8.0	-8.4	-11.5	-5.6	2.1	-2.7	7.1
Venezuela	0.0	6.6	3.8	5.9	-7.8	6.8	9.7	6.5	-1.0

Inflation (percent)

	1985	1986	1987	1988	1989	1990	1991	1992	1993
Argentina	385.4	81.9	174.8	387.7	4,923.3	1,343.9	84.0	17.5	7.4
Bolivia	8,170.5	66.0	10.7	21.5	16.6	18.0	14.6	10.4	9.3
Brazil	239.1	59.2	394.6	993.3	1,863.6	1,585.2	475.1	1,149.1	2,489.0
Colombia	22.3	21.0	24.0	28.2	26.1	32.4	26.8	25.1	22.6
Chile	26.4	17.4	21.4	12.7	21.4	27.3	18.7	12.7	12.2
Mexico	63.7	105.7	159.2	51.7	19.7	29.9	18.9	11.9	8.0
Peru	158.3	62.9	114.5	1,722.6	2,775.3	7,649.6	139.2	56.7	39.5
Venezuela	7.3	12.7	40.3	35.5	81.0	36.5	31.0	31.9	45.9

Source: IMF, ECLAC

Figure 5

Government Finance in Latin America:
Fiscal Deficit as Percent of GDP

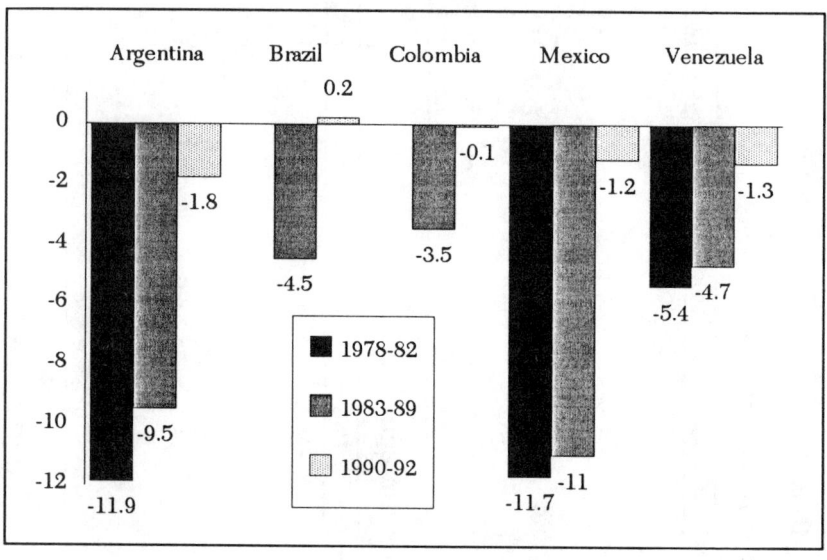

Trade Reforms in Latin America

More recently, the liberalization policies in the region have included trade reforms. As we noted above, Chile was the first country to begin extensive reforms in 1974 (see Figure 6). But in recent years other countries have joined in changing their trade policy regimes.

In Bolivia and Mexico, the unilateral liberalization of foreign trade began in 1986 and 1987, respectively, as part of a larger structural reform of these economies. Argentina started its liberalization process in 1989, and Colombia began major reforms in 1990. Peru and Brazil initiated their reforms processes in 1990 and 1991, respectively, while Uruguay did so in 1991 and Ecuador in 1993. In these different Latin American countries, the approach to trade liberalization has varied. In Bolivia, Colombia, Mexico, Argentina and Peru a "fast track" approach has been followed. Brazil, Uruguay and Ecuador have conducted their reforms at a slower pace.

Figure 6

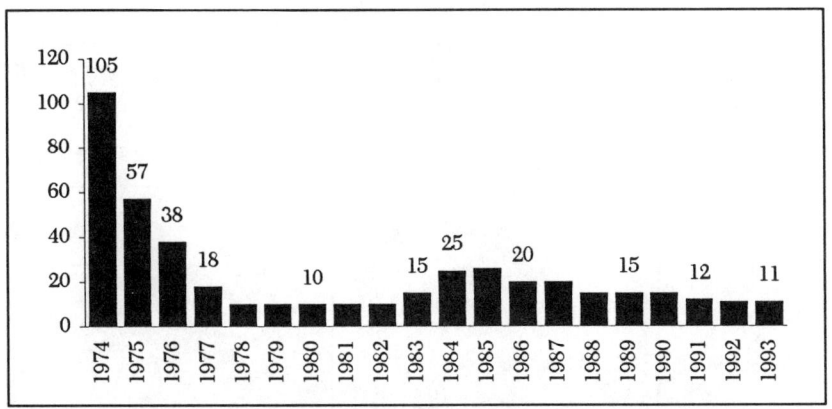

Chile: Average Annual Tariff Rate (percent)

In general, these various trade reforms have included a reduction of the anti-export bias, through lowered import duties, the devaluation of the exchange rate, and specific export promotion policies. The tariff cuts have led to a reduction of not only the maximum and average tariff rates, but also of the tariff dispersion (see Figures 7 and 8).

At the same time, quotas and other non-tariff barriers (NTB) have been almost completely removed by most countries. In some cases, quotas were replaced by tariffs that were subsequently reduced. It is important to note that many of the region's countries have also reformed their customs procedures, which had been used in the past as a form of NTB. In many cases, these were replaced with new agencies and simplified administrative procedures to facilitate trade.

Additionally, as part of these reforms, some countries have given greater independence to trade policy—reducing the discretionary decision-making power of the institutions involved in these policies—in an effort to avoid using trade policy as a substitute for sound macroeconomic policy.

Figure 7

**Latin America: Average Tariff and Non-Tariff Protection
(1985-1992)**

	Average Tariff Protection[*] (percent)		Average Coverage of NTB[**] (percent)	
	1985	**1991-1992**	**1985-1987**	**1991-1992**
Bolivia	20	8.0	25.0	0
Brazil	80	21.1	35.3	10
Chile	36	11.0	10.1	0
Colombia	83	6.7	73.2	1
Ecuador	50	18.0	59.3	n/a
Mexico	34	4.0	12.7	20
Peru	64	15.0	53.4	0
Uruguay	32	12.0	14.1	0

Source: S. Edwards (1993).

[*] Average total charges (tariffs plus paratariffs), unweighted.
[**] Unweighted.

In general, the rapid implementation and depth of the trade reforms represents a guarantee to the private sector of policy stability over time, reassuring the private firms that their adjustments to the new environment are necessary and inevitable.

From a general point of view one could say that these policies imply a dramatic change from the situation that prevailed in the 1970s and early 1980. Yet it is clear that their consolidation varies markedly from country to country. Apart from Chile, where a strong consensus upholds this economic model and there is great economic stability, only in Bolivia and Mexico can we say that these reforms are being consolidated. Colombia might arguably be added to the list. But Brazil and Venezuela are more complicated areas, where the political uncertainty makes it impossible to predict what sorts of policies will be implemented in the coming years. Finally, in Argentina and Peru

Figure 8

Latin America: Average Real Tariffs 1988-1993
(percent ad valorem)

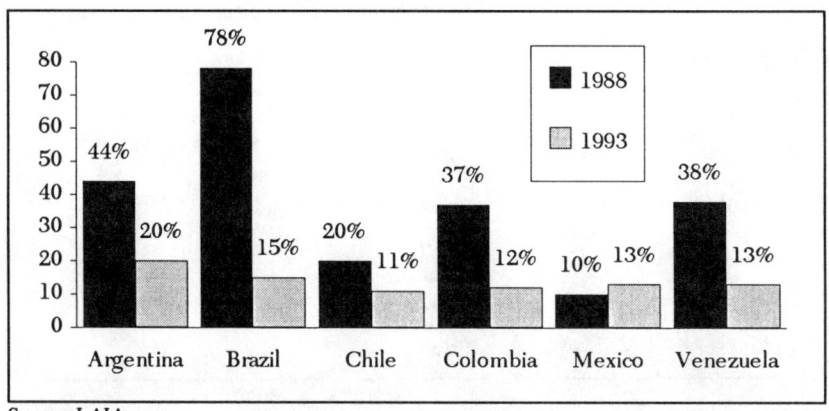

Source: LAIA

trade liberalization depends to a great extent on the success of the current stabilization efforts.

The clearest sign that liberalization is not complete is that in many of these countries we have seen different types of protectionism when "times get tough." One could conclude from this that greater attention needs to be given to reforms of administrative rules, which have more resistant to reform than other sectors in the economy, and to the anti-dumping procedures and countervailing duties which often end up being transformed into new forms of protection.

This can be seen in the region's risk classifications which, while significantly better than in the past, show that in many economies important tasks remain for the future (see Figure 9).

One of the key challenges for Latin American countries is thus to move ahead in the process of opening their economics, to give the private agents an environment of predictability in which they can take advantage of the pattern of incentives. This much will be needed to sustain the momentum of the reform process.

At the same time, greater progress should be made in complementary policies, as we shall see below.

Figure 9

International Risk Rating (October 1994)

	Moody's	Standard & Poor's
Argentina	B1	BB–
Brazil	B2	–
Chile	Baa2	BBB+
Colombia	Ba1	BBB–
Mexico	Ba2	BB+
Uruguay	Ba1	BB+
Venezuela	Ba2	B+

In any event, the reforms already mentioned have led to greater trade flows between Latin American countries. Intra-regional trade has increased substantially; between 1985 and 1993, intra-LAIA trade grew 225 percent, which compares very favorably with a 43 percent increase in Latin America's total exports.

Of course the reasons for this are not only commercial or economic. It is also fair to include geopolitical explanations, such as the recovery of democracy in the region and the fact that, since the early 1990s, lots of talking has been going on regarding economic blocs, and Latin American countries do not want to be left out in the cold.

Two points are worth stressing in summarizing the effects that the policies and reforms reviewed above have—or should have—on the economy as a whole.

First, it is important to remember that the impact of trade liberalization on economic growth is strong. International trade leads to improvements in productivity due to greater specialization, economies of scale because of the existence of bigger markets, exposure to foreign competition, and the more rapid implementation of technological innovations due to more extensive international contacts. Additionally, there is a positive welfare effect from the point of view of consumers, who gain access to less expensive and higher quality products.

But wider reforms are needed to achieve higher growth rates. While macroeconomic stability is necessary for private sector development, it is not sufficient. Uncertainty inhibits private sector activities; besides stability, the private sector needs also to be convinced of the continuity of policy regimes.

Recent studies in development economics suggest the importance of several other factors for growth to occur. The incentive framework, the security of property rights and the stability of institutions also play a crucial role in economic growth. Especially important is the creation of an environment that does not hinder the private sector and that allows elastic supply responses in the form of growth in output, savings and exports.

With greater stability, less uncertainty and orthodox policies that do not distort relative prices, savings and investment will become more attractive. This, together with a greater credibility in the long-term durability of the development model and a flexible labor market, is vital for higher growth rates in the short and long term.

At the same time, policies that create positive incentives in areas such as trade, finance and the regulatory environment are also important in determining private sector activity. Much has already been done in trade policy in Latin America, yet it is clear that many countries need to tackle many other reforms to improve the international movement of capital and people, and continue the liberalization of trade in goods where there still exist important "non-written" NTB.

The financial system, for its part, is vital for an effective intermediation between savers and investors. Here, greater transparency and less discretion is required, and an appropriate balance between financial liberalization and sound regulation and supervision needs to be found.

Lastly, rational regulatory policies, and what lies behind them—an institutional framework that guarantees property rights and an efficient and effective legal system—are important in encouraging private sector activity and job creation. Of course, further privatization and a lower and less distorted structure of taxes are also needed in all the Latin American countries.

Today in Latin America, too high a percentage of the population still lives in poverty; the only way for to foster individual progress and higher standards of living is through more productive occupations and better paid jobs. Recent evidence for Chile (Larrañaga 1994) suggests that 80 percent of the reduction in the number of poor families in Chile between 1987 and 1992, was explained by economic growth through more jobs and higher wages, and only 20 percent by central government social spending. This clearly demonstrates the social importance of economic growth and growth-enhancing policies.

The future of Latin America depends on the capacity to realize these reforms. Chile has showed that this is possible, and that is why it is the only country that has maintained a process of stable economic growth which has now lasted for more than 10 years.

After NAFTA, What . . . ?

It is to this picture that we add NAFTA. My premise in this paper is that NAFTA should be considered as the first step in the Enterprise for the Americas Initiative, which was laid out by President George Bush in 1990, and is an ambitious long-term program for free trade in Latin America and the Caribbean. That program consists mainly in creating a free trade zone in the Americas to stimulate foreign investment and canceling some fraction of the external debt of the countries that implement free market reforms.

This initiative, the single most important U.S. initiative in Latin America since the Alliance for Progress, has stirred action and debate in Latin America and the United States. Today there are a number of studies on the impact of a Latin American—U.S. free trade agreement, looked at from the point of view of the region as a whole, or from the perspective of subregional integration patterns or even individual countries.

In general, the reception to the Bush proposal in the region has been favorable, something that in itself is of great merit and which has much to do with the region's unilateral liberalization in recent years. Imagine what the response to such an initiative would have been only a decade ago!

But let me leave these analyses for a moment and make a few comments on what NAFTA represents. Although NAFTA is not perfect, nor for that matter an ideal trade liberalization, it is a good, broad agreement, covering such important new sectors as services and investment. At the same time, the fact that an agreement was finally reached when so many interest groups opposed it and campaigned against it, sends out a clear signal against one of the worst ills of our time, protectionism.

The experience of Chile, and Latin America more generally, shows that people can be imaginative and persistent when it comes to protecting certain sectors, infant industries or whatever. I would not like to defend some of the highly original NTBs that some Latin Americans countries use. But to be fair, I must say this problem is not unique to Latin America. Many developed countries also nowadays hide their protectionist policies in the regulations setting labor, environmental and quality standards.

To this date, the North American Free Trade Agreement has been operating for just shy of a year—we must keep in mind that it only started on January 1, 1994, and that a 15-year transition will precede the complete liberalization in trade of goods and services among the three member countries. So it is premature to evaluate its results. In any case, there seems to have been no shock or drama, as was predicted by many. And even though any evidence one may use is certainly biased in the sense that is statistically insignificant, there would seem to be a notorious increase in trade flows between the NAFTA member countries, particularly between Mexico and the United States.

But to go straight to the point of this section, after NAFTA, what . . . ? I think that NAFTA is the best available instrument to extend, deepen and consolidate the free market and export-oriented ideas and policies that have been at work in the region in recent years, and will thus lead to greater economic growth in the region.

The United States has a big stake in the stability and prosperity of the region for at least three reasons. First, it is clear that the U.S. has an economic interest in Latin America. Between 1981 and 1983, U.S. exports to the region fell by 43 percent, only recovering their 1980 levels in 1988. Yet today, Latin America is the fastest growing market in the world for U.S. exports.

Second, an improved economic situation in the region may help the U.S. to leave behind and overcome the loan defaults of the 1980s; at the same time, it could also mean that, ceteris paribus, there will be fewer incentives for waves of Latin American immigrants to go to the United States. Related to this is the fact that economic growth in Latin America, spurred by the extension of the free market, will contribute to social stability in the region through the eradication of poverty.

Finally, the U.S. has great interest in Latin America as a trading partner in a rapidly changing world economy where trade blocs are forming quickly and secure, international markets are necessary for growth.

Thus, I believe there are mutual interests in moving ahead with reforms in the region; for Latin America, there is the carrot of free trade with the U.S., and the domestic benefits of liberalization. And for the U.S., there is an economic and geopolitical interest in Latin America.

Let us consider in turn the implications of a U.S.-Latin America free trade agreement, versus the southwards extension of NAFTA.

In the world of economists, there is a relative consensus that in a second-best scenario, bilateral agreements are positive when, in their static effects, trade creation offsets trade diversion, and when there are positive dynamic effects. This is so because they may improve access to new markets, especially in a climate of tariff escalation. They create stable rules under which commercial relations take place, allowing for efficiency in the settlement of disputes and eliminating asymmetries derived from the different sizes of the trade partners. Lastly, they provide rules and guidance in new areas such as trade in services and investment flows.

Yet a proliferation of bilateral FTAs would bring with it great confusion, which could diminish existing and potential trade flows. It is clear that a great number of different FTAs, each with different rules, would create a situation where it may become difficult to manage the agreements. At the same time, the producers who want to export or import goods from different countries will have to keep in mind the existence of different agreements, which regulate their particular situations in different ways. In this sense, one can say that there is a social and economic cost attached to a proliferation of FTAs. Moreover, it seems reasonable to think that a proliferation of FTAs would only move us further away from the goal of multilateral liberalization, which is the stated objective of all these regional integration processes.

Still, as I said before, the NAFTA is a good agreement. Its rules are compatible with the norms set forth in the GATT agreements, and thus point toward multilateral trade liberalization. It is what is called an open agreement, which allows its member countries to keep their trade policy independence; it is an extensive agreement that includes other matters apart from import and export liberalization, such as services and investment flows between the member countries; it deals with sensitive subjects such as the labor and environmental problems in a sensible way, leaving them regulated in the side agreements; and it incorporates important provisions for dispute settlements. Of particular interest for most Latin American countries is the fact that access to NAFTA or an FTA with the United States may mitigate the tariff escalation otherwise faced in the U.S., and thus give greater incentives for an increase in higher value-added exports (see Figure 10).

Many of these benefits may not be achieved in bilateral agreements with the United States. And if any Latin American country eventually negotiates a better deal than what is stipulated in NAFTA, it seems reasonable to expect that the other member countries of NAFTA would step in to try to renegotiate NAFTA.

Particularly preoccupying is prospect of what could happen if specific American lobbies, domestic constituencies or organized pressure groups, unhappy with NAFTA, get a chance to include some parts of their agenda in an FTA between the U.S. and any single Latin American country. It is well known that many producer interest groups would be willing, and happy, to renegotiate their situation under NAFTA, in order to obtain greater protection from foreign exports.

The same concern is valid for the environmental and labor side agreements reached in NAFTA, which seem, from my point of view, satisfactory for most Latin American countries in the sense that they oblige them to uphold existing domestic legislation on these matters. I think that they should remain as side agreements of

Figure 10

Tariff Escalation on Chilean Exports to the United States (1990)

	Tariff Rate (%)		Percent of Total Exports to the U.S.
	Most Favored Nation	General System of Preferences	
Copper			
Unrefined, refined	1.00	1.00	15.63
Alloys, bars, rods, plates	1.20	0.00	1.57
Articles of copper	3.60	0.00	0.02
Fruits and Vegetables			
Fresh fruit and vegetables	1.20	1.00	31.30
Prepared fresh fruit and vegetables	10.80	10.62	4.06
Fish			
Raw fish	0.20	0.03	9.47
Prepared	5.10	0.08	0.72
Fish meal	0.00	0.00	0.44
Wood			
Wood	1.10	0.00	2.31
Raw wood	0.00	0.00	1.56
Plywood	1.48	0.00	0.48
Wood articles	6.80	0.00	0.27
Wood pulp	0.00	0.00	0.58
Paper	4.80	0.00	0.04
Wood furniture	3.20	0.00	0.68

Source: Butlemann and Frohmann (1992)

NAFTA, so as to avoid their use as arguments for trade protection (in the guise of opposing "social" dumping).

NAFTA, which is a very big and stable market (see Figure 11) is a known commodity, which offers reassurance that several subjects are well dealt with and will not be changed. At the same time, although NAFTA will not in my view move in the near future towards being a closed bloc, it offers a very good base from which to negotiate with other trade blocs.

For all of the above reasons, I think that a southwards extension of NAFTA, through the accession clause that the Agreement contemplates, is preferable to a series of bilateral agreements between the United States and Latin America. Moreover in the case of Chile only accession to NAFTA is beneficial. One must bear in mind that a bilateral FTA could be rejected by the Chilean Congress.

Figure 11

Market Size (1993)

	Population (millions)	GDP (millions U.S.$)	Total Exports (millions U.S.$)	Total Imports (millions U.S.$)
NAFTA	377.55	7,262,186	639,707	792,269
Canada	28.75	537,508	144,693	138,684
United States	257.59	6,377,900	464,773	603,438
Mexico	91.21	346,778	30,241	50,147
Andean Pact	96.15	154,252	30,003	29,505
Bolivia	8.06	5,586	930	1,206
Colombia	33.95	50,915	8,238	6,822
Ecuador	10.98	13,188	3,172	2,562
Peru	22.45	23,426	3,497	4,815
Venezuela	20.71	61,137	14,166	14,100
Mercosur	200.50	638,850	55,294	48,547
Argentina	33.49	241,362	13,090	16,786
Brazil	159.22	378,786	39,848	27,740
Paraguay	4.64	6,704	709	1,732
Uruguay	3.15	11,998	1,647	2,289

Source: IMF, ECLAC

Of course, as I said before, this does not mean that Latin America as a whole or as a bloc should immediately be accepted into NAFTA. NAFTA should accept the accession of new member countries independently and individually, and only if, and when, they truly deserve it.

Even though the economic effects for Latin America of entering NAFTA, or signing an FTA with the U.S. are not too great, there certainly are important collateral effects. NAFTA, it bears repeating, is a very big and stable market, with nearly 360 million consumers, and a per capita GDP of nearly $20,000 in the U.S., $19,000 in Canada, and $2,400 in Mexico. Certainly the size, purchasing power and stability of NAFTA make it attractive.

Yet different studies have shown that the static short-run trade effects from a U.S.-Latin American FTA would not be too significant. Due to the availability of information, let us focus on the effects of a U.S.-Latin America FTA, and not of an extension of NAFTA. The results are perfectly comparable for both alternatives, with the exceptions noted.

A relatively recent preliminary study on the trade between Latin America and the U.S. by Erzan and Yeats (1992), shows that if all Latin American countries signed bilateral agreements with the United States, in the short run the trade expansion would be relatively small—a 6.6 percent increase in Latin American exports to the U.S. if all U.S. tariffs are preferentially removed, which could reach 8.8 percent if hard-core tariff barriers were simultaneously removed as well—and unevenly distributed, with Mexico and Brazil taking 80 percent of the gains (see Figure 12).

This is due to the fact that in countries such as Bolivia, Chile, Ecuador, Peru and Venezuela, the number of goods affected by non-tariff barriers is very low, and less than 5 percent of exports are subject to "non-nuisance" tariffs in the United States. Of course, it is important to keep in mind that in general, tariff levels in the U.S. are low.

Yet most important of all, this study concludes that if the United States signs a series of individual free trade agreements with all of the Latin American countries, it could alter inter-regional trade patterns because the U.S. would have a major comparative advantage over other countries in the region, thus creating a great danger of trade diversion in the hemisphere. This means that if the Enterprise of the Americas Initiative resulted in a series of bilateral FTAs, a great opportunity to set the regional economy on a path to prosperity would be lost.

Figure 12

Projected Latin American Export Gains from Free Trade Areas (percentage growth in exports)

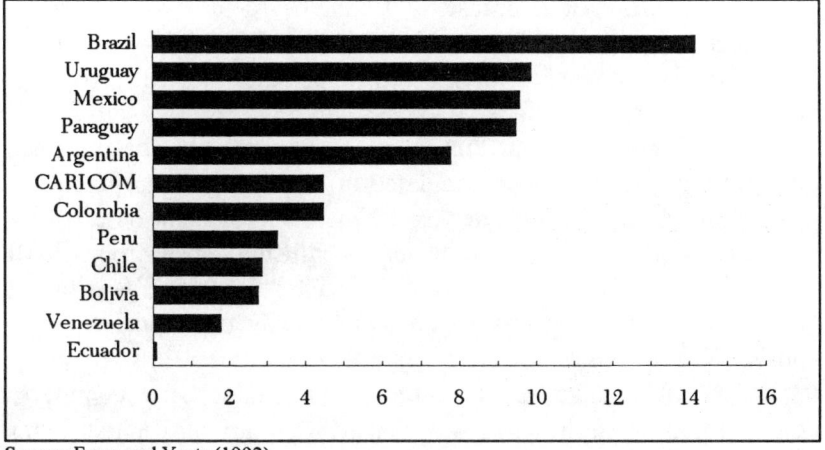

Source: Erzan and Yeats (1992)

Another study, prepared by the Confederación de la Producción y del Comercio of Chile (1992), suggests that if Chile signs an FTA with the United States, the benefits for this country in terms of exports expansion would not be too significant, being on average more important for exports that face higher escalated tariffs in the U.S. The most important positive effect of such an agreement for Chile would come from the image effect that is associated with the fact that if Chile enters NAFTA—it is because it really deserve it, and implicitly, there is a signal that it is a safe country to invest in. This "seal of quality" or trust in the Chilean economy may produce a reduction in the country's risk rating, which could significantly affect the decisions of many foreign investors who would like to come to invest in Chile. An exercise included in this study shows that a 0.5

percent reduction in the country risk rating could lead to an increase in investment equivalent to 2 percent of GDP.

Thus, although the short-term trade effects from a U.S.-Latin American FTA, are not too significant, the dynamic medium- and long-term effects related to investment flows, and increased productivity through greater international competition, are positive and important. Also, an extension of NAFTA may bring lower costs in terms of trade diversion.

I would now like to make a few comments on NAFTA's "entry fees." On various occasions, I have heard some arguments to the effect that the entry fees to NAFTA would be so high for some Latin American countries, they could hinder their growth prospects, since the burdens they will have to bear will be excessive.

I do not think that this is true. I have previously explained that many of the conditions stipulated in NAFTA are acceptable for many Latin American countries, so let me only comment on a couple of points where there may still be some confusion. Apart from what I have said before, I think that a great advantage of NAFTA is that it allows for gradual adjustments until completely free trade of goods and services is achieved. From a sectoral point of view, this will allow the more sensitive sectors of some Latin American economies to adjust gradually, in the same way that Mexico and the United States retained special treatment of some sectors—as exceptions in the negotiation and liberalization process.

I also think that it is necessary to shed light on some of the so-called dangers that some Latin American countries may face because of the wider reforms needed to make the country ready to meet NAFTA standards.

Stricter macroeconomic discipline, the correction of some economic imbalances, the stability of economic policies, and the constraints on the use of subsidies imposed by NAFTA, together with the minimum standards set in NAFTA on intellectual property rights, foreign investment, capital repatriation limits, and taxes, among others, are positive and good policies per se. They will help to consolidate the free market reforms in the region. Of course the adjustment processes may be hard, but as I commented before, NAFTA considers a gradual transition in several matters to be negotiable. This argument is also valid for trade liberalization, where the U.S. and some Latin American countries may start liberalizing their trade regimes from different initial protection levels.

By the same token, as I commented before, the environmental and labor standards imposed by NAFTA in the side agreements, are satisfactory and only imply the carrying out of national laws in these matters.

In short, I think that adjusting to the requirements imposed by NAFTA should pose no great problems for Latin American countries. Of course there will have to be an important resource reallocation in some countries, which while being very healthy in terms of economic efficiency, may make the transition difficult.

In any case, it is important to clearly understand that these re-forms will bring higher growth rates, more and better paid jobs and will thus contribute to eradicating extreme poverty and increasing social stability in these countries. In this way, the extension of NAFTA may have significant social benefits for the new countries that accede.

Finally, having explained what the next Latin American steps after NAFTA should be, I would like to consider what would happen if instead the U.S. closed its doors on Latin America.

It would be ironic if, after opening the door and offering great expectations, thus helping the implementation of brave reforms in the region, the United States discovers that it does not really have the re-solve to uphold its end of the implicit existing bargain.

I think it is important to consider the Enterprise for the Americas Initiative, the NAFTA, the several comments and speeches made by top U.S. foreign officials, and the various conversations be-tween Latin American and U.S. political leaders, as an implicit con-tract on the future extension of a free trade area in the Americas.

In economic organization theory, the role and importance of implicit contracts are now recognized to such an extent that the con-cept has given rise to very important recent academic research. The principal conclusion derived from these studies is that the breaking these contacts has a severe impact on all actors involved, principally because of the loss of trust.

The situation we are examining is equivalent. Apart from severe damage to Latin American-United States relations, there could be
a significant change in continental trade patterns, since Latin America
would start looking towards other markets, or inward. This is due to
the fact that in a global economy opportunities must be seized wherever one finds them, and if the North American market is closed, the
fast-growing Asian markets, or other Latin American markets, could
become good alternatives. This would, of course, negatively affect
current U.S.-Latin American trade.

At the same time—and this could be the most critical effect—the economic reforms in the region could be endangered because of the political loss of reputation of the reformers who promised
an FTA with the U.S. and a loss of prestige of free trade ideas in a
world which seems dominated by trade blocs. Additionally, the slow
positive results of the reform process could lead to more activist policies in the economies that might eventually endanger the hard-won
macroeconomic stability in many countries.

The newly elected Congress in the U.S., should soon give
Latin America a clear signal where the U.S. intends to go in its relations with the region. In the event that the Clinton administration
requests fast-track authority to negotiate an FTA with a Latin American country by the way of accession to NAFTA, we hope that the
Congress would grant it, and thus show its real commitment to free
trade and progress in the Americas.

In any event, Latin America must move forward independently in its reform process and avoid being dependent on U.S. policy
decisions, recognizing that the decision to take the road towards economic development is in their own hands.

Summary and Conclusions

In this paper I have reviewed the economic reforms that have
taken place in Latin America in recent years and studied the uneven
pace of consolidation of these reforms in different countries.

Although these reforms took place without the existence of
NAFTA, I have argued that expansion of NAFTA is a good way to
deepen and consolidate the free market reforms and economic integration in the continent. This is so because there are mutual benefits

for Latin American countries and the U.S. to be derived from a closer relationship.

Even though the reform process has accomplished a great deal in most Latin American economies, there is still much more to be done. Latin America needs to redouble efforts to liberalize its trade regimes and, more generally, to move towards free market policies. Such reforms should gain wide support because they will produce higher rates of economic growth, greater stability and wider prosperity in the region. NAFTA offers the correct incentives and thus is the best instrument for achieving these goals; what is more, NAFTA will provide important social benefits for the countries that join it.

Because a series of bilateral FTAs between Latin America and the U.S. could introduce significant protectionist measures that are not present in NAFTA, I have argued that these closer ties should take place through an expansion of NAFTA. At the same time, I have explained why the requirements imposed by NAFTA, though they may need to be phased in gradually (as NAFTA already provides) are not prohibitive for most Latin American countries, nor do they impose great costs. The new entrants to NAFTA, I have further argued, should be those Latin American countries that deserve it, in an independent judgment, and not the whole of the region as a bloc.

Finally I have examined what would happen if the U.S. should turn its back on Latin America, arguing that this is equivalent to breaking an implicit contract, and could severely damage U.S.-Latin American relations and endanger the reforms that have taken place in the region. In that event, there might arise a new set of economic relations between Latin America and other countries and continents, which could negatively affect U.S. interests in Latin America. That is why we hope that there will be political support in the U.S. for the extension of NAFTA.

Next Steps in Expanding NAFTA and Building Hemispheric Economic Integration: The View from Latin America (III)

LUIS-HERNAN PAUL

Chile's Position
Towards Its Accession to NAFTA

It is a privilege for me to take part in this conference, and I thank the Fraser Institute and the Hudson Institute for inviting me to address you today.

May I make it clear that my comments are my own personal opinions and do not represent the official position of the Chilean government. I should add, however, that in my country there are no major differences of opinion at present on the prospect of Chile joining NAFTA, so I can safely say that I believe my opinion to be fairly representative of my countrymen's position.

For those of you who are not very well acquainted with Chile, I will begin by giving you a few indicators of what Chile is and what it can offer in economic terms. Then I will describe the structure of our foreign trade, to give you an idea of the significance that joining NAFTA may have for Chile. Lastly I will discuss the fundamental principles under which Chile has established free trade agreements during the '90s.

Luis-Hernan Paul is senior fellow at the Centro de Estudios Publicos, Santiago, Chile at and Professor at the Business School of Universidad Catolica.

Tables 1 to 3 provide basic data on Chile and its economy. Our population is close to 14 million people. Our GDP was $45.6 billion in 1993 and this year should be over $50 billion. Our economy has slowed down a little bit and we are going to grow only between 4.0 and 4.5 percent in 1994. Next year we expect to get back to the 6 percent level that has been our average during the last 10 years Our currency has risen over 15 percent against the dollar this year.

Our exports have been growing an average of 10 percent per year during the last 10 years, and our imports are growing almost as fast. We have political stability, trade surplus, fiscal surplus, and are close to full employment. In sum, we are a small country that knows where it is going and likes to go fast. We are a good partner.

To put things in perspective, let me recall that the United States's GDP is 159 times greater than Chile's (Canada's 15 times and Mexico's 9 times). This means NAFTA's joint GDP is 183 times that of Chile. In terms of per capita GDP, the U.S. figure is 8.5 times higher and Canada's is 7.5 times, while Mexico's is similar to Chile's.

Beyond numbers, however, it is worth stressing that Chile as a country has a personality of its own. This is shown by the fact that our policies are generally supported by comprehensive analysis of the issues involved, which has often led us to choose innovative and unprecedented approaches. One example of this is our pension system, which is based on capitalization of individual accounts managed by privately operated pension funds.

This system began to operate in 1981 and is currently being copied in several parts of the world. I might add, too, that while free market policies are all the rage today, they were not so—at least not in Latin America—when Chile began to apply them in the mid-'70s. I am saying this to show that Chile's interest in joining NAFTA does not arise from a spirit of imitation but from the belief that it is an important initiative for Chile, Latin America and North America.

For a small economy such as ours, the optimum in the matter of trade is multilateral opening, where all countries liberalize trade of goods and services, capital flows and movement of individuals, with all of this is to be achieved as quickly as possible. This is what GATT aims at—and my country certainly supports it—but GATT procedures have proved too slow.

That is why Chile, apart from that broad agreement, has supplemented its strategy with parallel instruments. Since the mid-'70s Chile has established a successful unilateral opening policy, complemented in the '90s by a number of bilateral agreements. This strategy has proved beneficial for our economy and is necessary for our development; however, it is still not sufficient for continuing expansion.

Membership in NAFTA has the great advantage of reciprocal trade opening; that is, our goods would gain entry to NAFTA member countries on the same footing as their goods enter Chile. This would improve the access of our exports to one of their major markets, especially in the case of more highly processed items. Another advantage of joining NAFTA is that 27 percent of our imports already originate in those countries. The diversion of trade arising under the agreement would thus be minor. On the other hand, there is the effect of foreign investment, which, according to studies conducted in Chile, could be substantially more significant than the trade effect. In 1993, 63 percent of investments in Chile (about $1.7 billion) originated in the U.S. and Canada. Lastly, there is a further major benefit in consolidating the rules for trade and investments, establishing mechanisms for dispute settlement, together with liberalizing trade in financial and non-financial services.

Notwithstanding the benefits I have described, it should be remembered that joining NAFTA is not a life or death issue for Chile, because Chilean foreign trade is highly diversified (see Tables 4 and 5). The present members of NAFTA account for 20 percent of Chile's exports (the U.S. alone accounts for 18 percent), the Asia-Pacific countries account for 30 percent, the European Union 25 percent, South America 18 percent, and the rest of the world 7 percent. Regarding imports, NAFTA accounts for 27 percent (the U.S. alone 23 percent), Asia-Pacific countries 19 percent, the European Union 19 percent. South America accounts for 21 percent and the rest of the world 15 percent.

I do not wish to give the impression that accession to NAFTA is not a very significant issue for Chile. On the contrary, as I said earlier, I think it is, and we have given numerous indications of our interest in joining this trade agreement. At a seminar on NAFTA that we held at the Centro de Estudios Publicos just over a month ago, which was sponsored by Fraser Institute, Ricardo Vicuña, the chief member of the Chilean negotiating team for free trade agreements, said that Chile was like a bride waiting for hours for her bridegroom (the NAFTA members) to come to the wedding, and so was annoyed and bored. I would add that the bride is beginning to think seriously of returning home and going on with her normal life as a single girl (which means deepening unilaterally the integration to the world). Besides, as she is an attractive lady, she may very well find another groom more resolute than the first.

It seems this is not going to be necessary because we will have news about the groom soon. If we are invited to accede to NAFTA, various points will have to be specified and negotiated, and this should not take too long, because NAFTA rules are fairly clear. According to recent studies (e.g., *Chile's Readiness for NAFTA Accession*, by Fernñn Ibáñez and Felipe Larraín), only minor adjustments would have to be made to admit our country. To begin with, a new name would have to be devised.

In any event, Chile attaches importance to certain basic principles in the free trade agreements it enters into, which NAFTA meets reasonably well. First of all, our authorities have stated that they seek agreements adhering to the principles and rules established under GATT, expanding them beyond GATT wherever possible. Second, they wish Chile to retain a reasonable degree of autonomy in trade and tariff policies, which means freedom to move tariffs together with the rest of the world and to seek free trade agreements with other countries and regions. This is why Chile has chosen to negotiate free trade agreements rather than customs unions that require a common external tariff. Lastly, they have also stated that they seek to execute comprehensive agreements encompassing all the items on the trade agenda currently dealt with in GATT. This means covering, for instance, trade in goods and services, government procurement, technical standards, investment, intellectual property, dispute settlement, legislation on unfair competition, and labor and environmental issues. In this context, we agree to requiring member countries to monitor their own laws and keep systematic violation from becoming an artificial trade advantage.

Now, why admit Chile first rather than other countries? To answer this question I will rely on the conclusions of two well-respected experts from the U.S., Gary Hufbauer and Jeffrey Schott. They ranked the Latin American countries best prepared for possible accession to NAFTA, based on a series of variables, namely, price stability, fiscal discipline, foreign debt burden, currency stability, tariff level and structure, and political stability. Out of a maximum grade of 5 points, Chile rates 4.4, in first place among all Latin American countries, including Mexico.

Nonetheless, I do not believe that Chile should be the only country to join NAFTA. Moreover, it does not make sense to me to think of NAFTA as NAFTA nor of Mercosur as Mercosur per se. I see both agreements as stepping stones towards setting up a hemisphere-wide Free Trade Area in the medium and long term. An ambitious goal, certainly, but one that is well worth striving for.

Let me finish by saying that we have talked enough. The time has come to get things done.

Tables

Table 1

Chile: Basic Indicators

Population (1992)	(millions)	13.7
Area	(thousands of square kms.)	757
GDP (1993)	(U.S.$ billions)	45.6
Per Capita GDP (1993)	(U.S.$)	3,328
Inflation (1994)	(estimated average)	9.0
Unemployment (1994)	(percent of labor force, 9/94)	6.7
Life Expectancy (1992)	(years at birth)	71.0

Table 2

Sources of Growth
(real percentage rates)

	1985-90	**1991**	**1992**	**1993**	**1994**[a]
Consumption	2.8	9.1	11.5	6.3	2.5
Fixed Investment	12.2	-2.7	25.8	18.4	3.0
Domestic Expenditure	5.8	6.4	14.5	9.0	2.6
Exports	9.5	10.9	13.5	4.3	9.2
Imports	8.7	8.4	23.5	11.5	4.8
Gross Domestic Product	5.7	7.3	11.1	6.3	4.1
Inflation	2.1	12.7	12.7	12.2	7.4
Real Wages	1.2	4.9	4.5	3.3	5.8
Employment	5.2	0.7	4.1	5.5	-2.1
Current Account Ratio	2.7	-0.2	1.8	4.7	n/a
Investment Ratio	17.9	21.1	23.9	26.5	25.9
Public Sector Balance	1.0	2.2	2.6	1.8	n/a

[a] Through September

Table 3

1993: Growth by Sector

Sector	GDP Share	GDP Growth	Employment Growth
Agriculture & Forestry	6.9	1.6	-4.0
Fishing	1.1	0.8	n/a
Mining	8.2	0.9	6.0
Manufacturing	17.4	5.1	2.7
Utilities	1.4	4.3	8.9
Construction	5.6	14.0	19.0
Commerce	17.0	8.6	9.0
Transport & Communications	7.4	7.9	5.8
Other	35.9	14.5	-9.4
GDP	**100.0**	**6.3**	**4.5**

Table 4

Chilean Imports by Origin (1993)

	Millions of U.S.$	Percent of total
NAFTA	2,890.2	26.8
USA	2,477.4	23.0
Mexico	209.7	1.9
Canada	203.1	1.9
European Union	2,064.9	19.2
Germany	619.6	5.8
France	345.6	3.2
Italy	335.5	3.1
Asia-Pacific	1,987.9	18.5
Japan	882.6	8.2
Korea	343.2	3.2
Taiwan	212.5	2.0
China	185.4	1.7
South America	2,215.7	20.6
Mercosur	1,761.0	16.3
Brazil	1,060.2	9.8
Argentina	580.9	5.4
Andean Pact	454.7	4.2
Other	1,612.7	15.0
Total	10,771.4	100.0

Table 5

Chilean Exports by Destination (1993)

	Millions of U.S.$	Percent of total
NAFTA	1,847.1	19.6
USA	1,655.2	17.6
Mexico	130.8	1.4
Canada	61.1	0.1
European Union	2,396.0	25.4
Germany	554.4	5.9
France	486.5	5.2
Italy	373.7	4.0
Asia-Pacific	2,802.1	29.8
Japan	1,502.3	16.0
Korea	413.4	4.4
Taiwan	407.7	4.3
China	183.5	1.9
South America	1,656.0	17.6
Mercosur	1,089.2	11.6
Brazil	588.9	6.3
Argentina	407.1	4.3
Andean Pact	566.8	6.0
Other	715.0	7.6
Total	9,416.2	100.0

The Economic Integration
of Our Hemisphere

AMBASSADOR EVERETT ELLIS BRIGGS

From the titles of the several sessions of this important gathering, and from what we have heard so far, it seems evident that all of us—most of us, anyway—share a common vision of where our Hemisphere should be headed as we approach the 21st century: full partners in trade; an association of free and prosperous democracies.

These are the aims of the Council of the Americas, a business organization founded in 1963 by David Rockefeller and a group of like-minded American business leaders, in reaction to President Kennedy's Alliance for Progress. The Council from its inception has been dedicated to free trade, private enterprise and to the promotion of business ties throughout the Hemisphere.

The emphasis in the Alliance was on government promotion of development through what was euphemistically called "cooperation." Under this formula the less developed agreed to cooperate with the United States by accepting our handouts—in the form of economic assistance—and accepting, too (at least in theory) our lead in cold war foreign policy. The prevailing wisdom at the time prescribed state intervention and import-substitution as the quickest way to economic progress. Our own AID programs were fashioned to support this approach. In the process, the economies of many

---

Ambassador Everett Ellis Briggs is President of the Americas Society and the Council of the Americas.

countries became highly distorted, and a number of AID recipients became permanent pensioners of the United States.

By the end of the cold war, many painful lessons had been learned—at least in Latin America, if not in academia at home (where intellectuals to this day often remain frozen in their adolescent, socialist fixations). Like welfare programs here, so-called cooperation, in most instances, did not bring the expected benefits, except to the burgeoning bureaucracies it spawned. State-managed economies were failures, and to the extent U.S. aid prolonged the agony, it doubtless did more harm than good.

Gradually, led by Chile—prompted by the debacle of Allende—the realization dawned in Latin America that socialism was a fraud, while unfettered markets were the key to economic well-being, to meeting the social needs of the populace, and to sustaining democracy.

Our country for years had resisted the Latins' entreaties for "trade, not aid." And rightly so, for a while anyway, since from the Latin American standpoint this would have meant simply swapping one type of one-way "cooperation" for another, given the high protective tariffs, subsidies and crippling regulations devised by mercantilist elites in league with corrupt strongmen throughout much of the region.

But as we all know, we now find ourselves in a dramatically changed setting—one of breathtaking opportunities.

For the fourth consecutive year, Latin America's GDP has grown by almost 4 percent—a rate which soon will exceed that of East Asia. U.S. exports to Latin America are increasing at three times the global rate—soaring by 14 percent a year between 1985 and 1992, with manufactured goods accounting for the greatest share. Next year, our exports to Latin America may well surpass those to Western Europe, just as our exports to Mexico nearly exceed those to Japan. The Western Hemisphere, in fact, is fast becoming our biggest market, with a total population soon to reach 800 million and a GDP of $13 trillion.

What has happened, of course, is that there has been a major shift in economic development strategies by Latin American countries over the past decade—from failed, inward-looking, import-substitution stagnation to efficient, outward-looking, export-oriented growth. As trade liberalization has proceeded, the average effective tariffs of Latin American countries have fallen from 26 to 13 percent. The new GATT regime will lower these still further.

Governments do not trade; private sector businessmen do. Trade liberalization and the elimination of tariffs, quotas and bureaucratic interference in general enlarge the area of human freedom. Business decisions are prompted by market forces, not politics, ideology, or special interests. Corruption, which feeds on over regulation, is curtailed.

Freedom of association and the ability to conduct business affairs openly should, in fact, be regarded as basic human rights.

The Council of the Americas is dedicated to advancing this proposition. It has long championed two sets of goals:

- Promoting economic integration in the Hemisphere, with the aim of creating a Hemisphere-wide free trade and investment area by the year 2000; and

- Encouraging economic restructuring, from closed, low productivity, import-substitution oriented economies to open, high productivity, globally competitive export-oriented economies.

The most significant step toward achieving these goals was the NAFTA—one of the most important trade policy achievements of the past two decades, of the same order of importance for hemispheric relations as the GATT Uruguay Round is for global trade. NAFTA's real significance is its potential for expansion. NAFTA's underlying principles—grounded in over four decades of international trade law and practice, are ideally suited for this purpose. They are readily adaptable to encompass the diversity and independence of this hemisphere's community of nations. What is needed now is action by the three NAFTA members to agree on an accession code based on NAFTA standards, and then invite others to join. Chile, by general agreement, is first in line, and ready.

Chile is clearly the regional leader in long-term macroeconomic stabilization. Its outstanding record of sustained economic growth is unsurpassed. Furthermore, Chile has, as part of its comprehensive, market-based, economic reform program, one of the most transparent and nondiscriminatory trade regimes in the region. Its trade is globally diversified and expanding rapidly, emphasizing that trade is a key component in rapid growth policies designed to expand incomes across the society—and to address social needs in general. For those worried about labor and environmental practices, Chile's appear to be NAFTA-consistent. I understand that President Clinton is expected to announce very soon that the three NAFTA members are, in fact, prepared to open accession negotiations with Chile.

Latin American governments in the past often deliberately excluded U.S. participation in regional trade arrangements. Most now say they would welcome it. If the United States and its NAFTA partners should fail to offer them a means to climb aboard the NAFTA bandwagon, the Latin Americans will have no choice but to associate themselves with others.

This will not be hard, given the imperative of trade in the modern world. A case in point: last month Mercosur Foreign Ministers met with Jacques Delors of the European Union to discuss the creation of a free trade zone between the two economic blocs, with negotiations to begin early next year. The EU heads of state are scheduled to discuss this prospect at their quarterly meeting in Germany on December 10. The timing of this meeting with that of the Summit may not be entirely coincidental.

What is needed is to simplify the accession process by making it as transparent as possible. Chile, as I said, has a privileged place and stands first in line. This is to some extent symbolic, both for Chile and for NAFTA, since Asia, not NAFTA, has become Chile's top trading partner. But Chile's accession sets the precedent for the rest of the continent; and the fact that Chile is itself a global trader is important to NAFTA's eventual prospects.

In many respects, trade liberalization under NAFTA has gone far beyond what the GATT Uruguay Round accomplished on a global basis. NAFTA complements and extends GATT actions. NAFTA is the leader, providing valuable guideposts for the future evolution of the trading system both in the Hemisphere and globally. Opening NAFTA to new members will make the advantage of trade liberalization more evident to all.

And one of those we should care about is itself already a world-class global trader—the Colossus of the South—Brazil.

Brazil and the United States: for years we were close allies, the two big giants who enjoyed a genuinely special relationship as partners, not rivals. The relationship soured in the Carter years and has yet to be restored.

Brazil, estranged from the United States, seems to have developed a different vision from ours. Its spokesmen talk (in what sounds like EC-speak) of broadening and deepening Mercosur, by attracting other, existing South American groupings and hardening Mercosur's shell—against outsiders—creating a South American common market with guess who in charge. Brazilians have talked of creating a SAFTA to balance NAFTA, and maybe when some sort of balance is reached, they might be ready to discuss integration with us.

But Brazil, like the United States, is not monolithic, and there may be other views. Many Sao Paulo business leaders seem to be attracted to the notion of a Hemisphere-wide free trade area, sooner rather than later.

We at the Council of the Americas like to boast about the role of one of our standing committees—the Mexico-U.S. Business Committee—in doing the spadework that gave a real boost to our respective NAFTA negotiators. Is there a model there for future U.S.-Brazil trade relations? The Council already enjoys close ties with AACCLA and the U.S. Section of the Brazil-U.S. Business council, and it might be useful in the days ahead to build a stronger association between U.S. and Brazilian business sectors to examine jointly how to speed up the process of integration, as was done in the pre-negotiating period with our Mexican counterparts.

A globally-attractive NAFTA—open not only to Chile and our other Western Hemisphere neighbors, but eventually to more distant candidates as well—might prove more appealing to Brasilia than a more restricted North American-managed club.

We hope the Clinton administration, and its successors, will work with Brazil to reestablish the special relationship that once existed. We should quickly welcome Chile into NAFTA, as this will undoubtedly encourage other likely candidates, several of whom are now close to meeting NAFTA standards. But Brazilian membership is crucial to our goal of Hemispheric integration, and should be one of Washington's top priorities, starting now.

Turning to this week's other Summit, the one in Miami, the Council, together with AACLA, and in consultation with several other organizations, including DEAL—and in response to supplication from allies in the Clinton administration—has worked assiduously to influence the Summit's agenda and, hopefully, its outcome.

On the agenda, we have sought to persuade the White House to make trade, not social problems, the centerpiece of the Summit. We produced a White Paper that we distributed widely. Its central premises are:

- that the rule of law and freedom of choice—both in economics and in politics—are basic rights;

- that private sector economic activity is the engine of growth; and

- that sustained economic growth is essential for any agenda for the Americas to succeed.

Based on those premises, we offered the following specific policy recommendations for the Summit:

- that the countries commit themselves to negotiating a hemispheric free trade area by the end of this century;

- that they agree that the best path to hemispheric economic integration is the expansion of NAFTA, with its principles the basis for trade and investment liberalization;

- that they commit to establish and maintain sound macroeconomic and microeconomic policies—the chief prerequisites for hemispheric FTA negotiations;

- that the trade ministers meet periodically to keep up the pace of integration; and

- that countries adopt appropriate legislative procedures to be able to approve a WHFTA expeditiously and as negotiated.

In fact, I am pleased to say, a fair amount of this will indeed take place. We have learned today that the Summit will call for the creation of a "Free Trade Area in the Americas" (FTAA) and for negotiations to be complete by the year 2005. Substantial progress (meaning all but the hardest cases) is to be expected by the year 2000. How this happy state of affairs will be made to come about is less clear, although an outline of a method is spelled out.

The OAS Special Committee on Trade will be tasked with undertaking a comprehensive study of all the trade arrangements in the Western Hemisphere. There are some 23, including NAFTA. The purpose of this effort, of course, is to devise a way to bring all of them together. Meanwhile, existing trade fora are to be used in bilateral and plurilateral discussions to compare and contrast the trade and microeconomic regimes of countries by a set of criteria largely drawn from the precepts of NAFTA. Finally, progress will be directed and monitored by the trade ministers, who will meet formally in June 1995 and March 1996. This process is to begin in January.

My comment would be: The process seems a little diffuse and without a central driving force and direction. A simple NAFTA accession mechanism would have worked more effectively. Nevertheless, what has been agreed upon seems workable if we all have the will to make it work, and that will be the Council's intention and purpose.

Two issues had earlier blocked consensus among the countries. The United States had in fact proposed that the quickest, most efficient way to expand trade was by way of a NAFTA accession mechanism. But the Brazilian government opposed a NAFTA-centered approach, and the Central Americans, fearful of being left behind, also balked. The question of accession has, therefore, been set aside by the Summit. Accession to NAFTA can, of course, still take place, and it should. As I have already pointed out, Chile is the outstanding example.

The second issue concerned the Clinton administration's single-minded insistence that labor and environmental issues be explicitly linked to trade liberalization. Reportedly all of the Latin American countries rejected this. Only Canada supported us. As a sop to Washington, the declaration to be signed in Miami will contain only a watered-down reference to the environment (based on language in the Rio Agreement), and a sentence or two on labor cribbed from the GATT.

Whatever the Summit produces, the Council of the Americas and our 270 corporate members will remain unswerving in our goal: the economic integration of our Hemisphere through a hemisphere-wide free trade agreement, as soon as possible. We'll work for this, starting next year, with the campaign for securing the Administration the fast track authority it needs to lead the process—without labor or environmental conditionality. And, meanwhile, we'll do whatever we can to support Chile's candidacy in NAFTA.

We'll be urging others, and particularly the new, Republican-controlled Congress (whose Contract with America needs a free trade clause), to forge ahead and to build on the bipartisan successes that NAFTA and GATT represent.

The opportunities of which I spoke—in today's modernizing Latin America—beckon. Remember, in matters of trade, you are either moving forward or you are falling behind. The United States as the world's free trade leader really has no choice.

Security and Stability—Keys to Enhanced Trade in Latin America

AMBASSADOR JON GLASSMAN

It is a great challenge being here and filling in for both the former Vice President of the United States and the former Secretary of State.

I thought it would be interesting to move from what we have been talking about heretofore, which has been basically the future of trade agreements and issues of macroeconomic stability, and go over to the issue of military security and political stability. There is a real logic for discussing these issues.

The logic I think was expressed very well by David Malpass yesterday when he was talking about the fact that what we are looking for is not trade agreements, but trade itself. In other words, the bottom line is not the question of whether we go forward to greater hemispheric integration in terms of trade agreements, but rather that trade actually occur. And security and stability lie at the root of this.

Number one, as we look at the history of Europe, we know that security considerations reinforced economic integration. That is to say that the desire of the United States and the European allies to cooperate on defense gave the initial impulse for the formation of the European Coal and Steel Community, which led to the formation of the European Community. In turn, ongoing trade integration allowed

---

Ambassador Jon Glassman holds the Department of State Chair, Industrial College of the Armed Forces, National Defense University.

security cooperation to be consolidated. The economic side inevitably influences the security side and vice versa.

Number two, we also know the great effect that stability has on investment. In the current world, capital is mobile. We live in a very intensely competitive world, and capital will go where opportunities exist. We heard yesterday about the great extent to which increased trade in Latin America has been motivated by foreign investment. Intra-company trade, trade within one company or one production unit across national borders, in some of the countries accounts for 50-60 percent of the total increase in recent years. So we can say with good justification that trade follows investment. Investment, of course, follows stability. This makes the issues of military security and political stability keys to trade growth.

Number three, we should remember that President Clinton is the third successive American President who has ordered a military incursion in a Latin American country. I don't think American forces have been used so frequently in any other region in the world. That fact shows that regardless of political ideology, the issues that move Latin America frequently have led to the use of extreme pressure or force by the United States. This in turn affects the perceived stability of the area and its perceived attractiveness for investment.

It is clearly important, therefore, for us to examine carefully the issues of military security and political stability. I want to review briefly how Latin America looked to us during the era of the Cold War, how it looks today as expressed in the current Administration's national security philosophy, and speculate how future developments will impact the stability of the area.

First of all, during the Cold War period, the United States was concerned about the deployment of hostile forces that could strike the United States. The Cuban Missile Crisis, gave substance to this concern. Was it a real problem? We know that in the case of Cuba, medium range ballistic missiles were deployed, bringing the cities and bases of the United States into range. We now know, based on disclosures since the end of the Cold War, that nuclear weapons were in Cuba at that time. We also know, based on the disclosures by Soviet military people at conferences that Harvard University has held, that Soviet commanders had the flexibility to use tactical nuclear weapons

if an American invasion of Cuba had occurred during the missile crisis. So in those days, Latin America, because of its propinquity, its
nearness to the United States, did represent a real security problem for
us.

Second, the United States from World War II on was concerned with the deployment of hostile forces in this hemisphere that
could block our reinforcement of the Eurasian periphery. During
World War II, German submarines operated in the Caribbean and
American ships were sunk there. During the entire Cold War period,
we were concerned that a permanent Soviet base would be established
here from which Soviet naval or air assets could interfere with our
capability of reinforcing the periphery. Our security frontiers were on
the edges of Europe and Asia, and because we were a continental
power we had to deploy our power afield.

Third, during the Cold War, National Security Document 68
of 1950 formed the basis of our perception that the loss of any country in the world to Communism was a strategic loss to the United
States. We were constantly preoccupied with the change of political
alignments in Latin America. You will recall Guatemala in 1954,
where the United States supported covert action to supplant the Ar-
benz regime, and the military intervention in the Dominican Republic
in 1965, and of course the Grenada invasion of 1983. All were basically designed to prevent the change in the political balance in the
world and, more specifically, Latin America.

Now with the end of the Cold War, with the demise of the
Soviet Union and perhaps the fatal weakening of Cuba, all these cal-
culations, all these factors which I have mentioned above, have probably become obsolete. They are no longer considerations or motives
preoccupying the United States or driving it towards military intervention in the Hemisphere.

What is the current Administration's outlook on national security in the world at large? Is Latin America a focus of concern? The
Administration's national security strategy is spelled out in a new
document entitled "A Strategy of Engagement and Enlargement,"
issued in July 1994. It says that the three main threats to U.S. national
security are the countries of Iran, Iraq and North Korea. It says that
these are important regional threats, because only in those areas can

powerful forces be generated which cannot be counterbalanced without the United States entering the equation. So, in terms of security, military danger, the focus is on Northeast Asia and the Middle East. The Administration also points to Europe, for it says that we must preserve NATO as a guarantee against a resurgence of aggressive policy in Russia and as a vehicle for managing ethnic conflicts such as we have seen in the former Yugoslavia. So, again, despite the demise of the Soviet Union, despite the change in world circumstances, our security concern focuses on the periphery of Europe and Asia.

The Administration does, however, introduce one new consideration, which has heretofore not figured in U.S. national security documents. That is the question of refugee outflow. This is probably provoked by concern over the Haiti situation, but for the first time in history that I am aware of, the Administration has said that countries that can produce refugee outflow can represent a national security threat to the United States. I should point out they refer not only to the United States, but also to refugee outflow to our allies, referring to the possible rise of Islamic fundamentalism in North Africa, etc.

As we have seen this year, because of crises in Haiti and Cuba, there have been several incidents of large-scale refugee outflow. The Administration has had to react and pursue measures of detention, which probably will not be sustainable for a long period of time. But this is a new area of concern in the post-Cold War world in which Latin America figures prominently.

Let us now look for a moment to the future, on the basis of pure logic and speculation. How could Latin America threaten the United States or create security threats for the United States in the post-Cold War world?

Number one, an obvious possibility is the proliferation of missile and long range aircraft capabilities. This allows countries whose weapons formerly could not reach the U.S. to bring the U.S. into range. Certainly, this could be important because of Latin America's contiguous position to the United States. It could affect our interests.

Number two, actions endangering our economic well being and our nationals. Obviously, we are going to have more investment interests, we are going to have more trading interests, we are going to have more U.S. nationals located in Latin America. We will discuss that in a moment.

Number three, domestic turbulence and repression, which could provoke refugee outflow. We have already seen this in Haiti and Cuba this year. We could see it in other nations if economic stability were in danger. Reversals of democracy are also a possible threat. At the Miami Summit, they're going to reiterate the need for the nations of the Hemisphere to defend democracy.

In the last three or four years, democracy has become enshrined as the only legitimate form of government in this Hemisphere. Just as in Europe after the Napoleonic wars, the monarchs of that age and the Holy Alliance vowed to defend monarchy as the only legitimate form of government. We now have decided, collectively in this Hemisphere to defend democracy as the only legitimate form of government. Therefore, a reversal of democracy through a coup now becomes a threat to the nations of the Hemisphere, defined as such at the Hemispheric Summit this week.

Lastly, let's turn to the question of narcotrafficking and narco-related interests. Should narco-related interests assume predominance in any country, this would be viewed as a threat to the United States's interests. We have seen the case of Noriega, which developed somewhat spontaneously, but Noriega was defined as a threat to the United States, was incarcerated, and remains incarcerated. The United States, because of its own internal turmoil and because of crime within the United States, will continue to make narcotics a big issue.

There is a growing consciousness in Latin America that narcotics are becoming not only an issue of criminality, but also an issue of national security. Consider the inaugural address of President Zedillo in Mexico, in which he said "Drugs are the gravest threat to Mexican national security; the gravest threat to the health of society; and the bloodiest source of violence." That means narcotics has moved from an issue of criminality, of social peace, to an issue of security concern. The reason President Zedillo has raised this issue is because of the suspected links of drug traffickers to terrorism, and certainly the killing of Ruiz Massieu. Drug trafficking has become a big issue, and a big danger.

That being said, what are the threats or potential conflicts that one could imagine in Latin America? Number one, international conflict. But the risk of international conflict in Latin America is down at the lowest point that we have seen in years. Ongoing border conflicts and arms competition between Argentina and Brazil, between Argentina and Chile, between Colombia and Venezuela, Peru and Ecuador, and among the Central Americans are very tranquil now. This is a marked change from the past. Border conflicts and potential for conflicts because of frontier difficulties are down. Arms competition is down. Because of budget restrictions, the only active military modernization effort taking place in Latin America today is in Chile.

Number two, the danger of proliferation of nuclear, chemical, and biological weapons and modern aircraft and missiles is down. As you know, Argentina has abandoned the Condor II missile project and has joined the Missile Technology Control Regime. Brazil is also adhering to the export guidelines of the Missile Technology Control Regime. Argentina and Chile have ratified the treaty of Tlatelolco which bans nuclear weapons in Latin America, and Brazil is taking the final measures to put it in force. So we can say, for the moment, the danger of proliferation of both long range systems of delivery and of chemical, biological, and nuclear weapons is down in Latin America. And because of budget restraints, the respective militaries do not have the means to modernize their capabilities.

In terms of nuclear programs, Brazil and Argentina have both reached a full scope safeguard agreement with the International Atomic Energy Agency and in the Mendoza Declaration, Brazil and Argentina have renounced chemical and biological weapons. So those are good signs in terms of moderation.

However, guerrillas continue to exist and are active in a few Latin countries. They are operating in Mexico, Guatemala, Peru, and in Colombia. But if we look at the dangers that these guerrillas represent, it is much less than we might imagine. With the demise of the Soviet Union and with the absence of financial resources in Cuba, these guerrilla forces no longer represent a transnational danger as they arguably did in the 1980s. Their influence is localized, and because of ongoing negotiations and effective governmental actions, their danger to societies is remarkably down. The change in Peru, of course, has been the most notable.

Narcotrafficking, on the other hand, continues to grow as a menace. I mentioned President Zedillo's statement at his inauguration. We know that outgoing Brazilian President Itamar Franco has said that this is the year that they must fight narcotics. The Brazilian army has been sent into the slums, the *favelas* of Rio, to try to curb narcotrafficking. The problem with narcotrafficking, particularly in small countries, is that the returns are so high that they will begin to influence political contests.

In the small country from which I have just come, Paraguay, the cost of a presidential campaign is only $12 million. To a narco-trafficker, that's pocket change. The narcotraffickers are in a position to buy political allies and to decisively influence presidential elections. This is really the only bad news on the horizon we have so far covered.

Economic reforms have caused disturbances in some countries. You remember in Venezuela in 1992, there were two military coup attempts. We had some local disturbances in Argentina. We had the Chiapas uprising in Mexico. These are both products of the fundamental economic problems that the region suffered in the 1980s and a reflection of the adjustment problems associated with economic reform, which we will discuss briefly in a moment.

I think the most promising thing that is occurring in Latin America now is that we may be entering an era in which international conflict among the states of Latin America may become unthinkable. In other words, if you look back at our own relations with Europe, you see that we had war plans against Great Britain up until the beginning of this century. Today we cannot imagine, there is nobody in this room who can imagine, the United States going to war with Great Britain. We have made that psychological transformation. By the same token, that transformation has occurred in Western Europe. Because of both security cooperation and economic integration, the possibility of a French-German war, the central theme of much of the history of this century is really something that cannot be conceived of today. We may now be at that stage in Latin America, where the possibility of international conflict is something of the past. This is very important in terms of the basic fundamental stability that we see today.

The ongoing economic changes in Latin America buttress this conclusion. If we look at trade among the individual countries of Latin America, we find that in 1960, it was only 8.8 percent of total Latin American trade. By 1990, that figure had reached 13 percent, and it is now growing rapidly. Intra-regional trade within Latin America grew by 79 percent between 1988 and 1992 . So in other words, the Latins are trading more with each other, and this interdependency will fortify and reinforce security as it did in Europe. In addition, in terms of other figures that were cited in yesterday's speeches, Congressman Ibarbia mentioned that trade among the Mercosur states, Argentina, Brazil, Paraguay, and Uruguay, increased by 58 percent in 1993. That is a remarkable increase. Among the countries of the Andean Pact, Colombia, Venezuela, Peru, Ecuador and Bolivia, trade has expanded over the last three years by 20 percent annually. So we see these nations coming together, and consequently the likelihood that their militaries or politicians will promote conflict between them decreases.

In terms of integration with the United States, Dr. Roett mentioned the inroads of the European Union in the southern cone of South America. But if we look at the entire continent, in fact, trade is being directed away from Europe and towards the United States. In 1980, for example, 40 percent of the region's exports went to the United States. By 1990, that had gone up to more than 50 percent. During the same period, Latin exports to the European Union declined from 48 percent to 22 percent of total exports. So, the exports of Latin America are increasingly directed towards the United States. That is the trend.

55 percent of imports into Latin America came from the United States in 1990, which was an increase from the 50 percent of 1980. Exports from Europe to Latin America went from 30 percent in 1970 to a 20 percent share in 1990. Japan made no significant new inroads during that 20 year period. Between 1987 and 1992, Latin imports from the United States grew faster than U.S. sales to any region in the world. So, both U.S. exports to Latin America and Latin exports to the United States and Canada are growing. The direction of

trade is north-south, and this in turn will create links of interdependency that will argue against the rise of nationalist, anti-U.S., anti-Canadian nationalism in Latin America.

We have talked about the fact that U.S. exports to Latin America are mainly manufactured goods. U.S. exports to Latin America more than doubled between 1985 and 1993, rising from $30 billion to $79 billion. In other words, we are talking about a two and a half fold increase since 1985. But, you must remember, that of the $79 billion of U.S. exports, $50 billion of that will go to Mexico. So it is heavily Mexico-centered, but the trend is up for the rest of Latin America too.

The same trend is true of financial flows. As we discussed yesterday, U.S. investment in Latin America is now increasing two and a half times faster than in the rest of the world. In 1992, just to cite one year, U.S. investment went up 16.6 percent. So, both trade and financial flows are linking North to South producing more interdependency and more stability. Now, all of these figures are very impressive, but how does Latin America weigh in our global equation? How important is it?

I have the feeling that some Latins will say that it's great that all this business is going on, but we don't want to be the end-all of U.S. economic prosperity. We don't want to be the target of U.S. intervention to save this economic base. Well, the fact is, while trade is growing dramatically, it is still only a small part of the U.S. global total. It constitutes about 16 percent of our global exports and about 17 or 18 percent of our global investment. Latin America is growing and important to us, but it is not the end-all for U.S. prosperity.

What could be the threats to security and stability? What could be the threats to these interests? What could be the threats to the democracy and prosperity of our Latin partners? Obviously, we are sensitive this year to the questions of Haiti and Cuba. We have seen how repression in both cases generated refugee outflow, which in turn generated U.S. responses in terms of economic or military pressure. This is good medicine for local problems, but it is bad medicine for the reputation of Latin America. Obviously, if Cuba were to become a democracy, if we could convince all the Latin American militaries to stay out of politics, that would be the best advertisement for investing in Latin America, and that is what, I am sure, you are all striving for.

The other systemic danger, however, beyond this question of repression, is the issue of interdependency between the Latin countries. During the Cold War, we often talked about the domino effect. We talked about the fact, that if one country went Communist, perhaps the incentives would exist for another country to go Communist. If we transfer that train of thought to the economic side of the equation, there is also a domino effect that could exist in the economic realm. That is to say, that because of the growing interdependence between the Latins, a collapse in one Latin country, either because of the image of that collapse or because of the economic effects of that collapse on trade, could promote a series of failures, just as a bank failure sometimes leads to another bank failure. In other words, interdependence breeds vulnerability in addition to prosperity. So the question is, what could cause a failure in one Latin country, or would set off some kind of chain of failed circumstances?

Basically, you could think of a problem involving, say, rising interest rates in the northern hemisphere, recession, a fall of commodity prices, persistence of Latin trade deficits, or an oil crisis. All these could possibly lead to a domino effect. If something like this were to occur, the guerrilla elements, populist elements, and narco elements would all prosper and this could breathe life into a vicious circle of circumstances that could cause problems. A particular concern in these circumstances would be if a series of problems like this caused the private capital inflow to Latin America to dry up. The change in Latin American circumstances since the 1970s is that prosperity and growth depends much more now on private capital flows, not on official flows, not even on commercial banks or sovereign lending. It is private capital flows in the form of direct investment, equity purchases, etc.

Some have argued, however, that a part of this flow is due to the wave of privatizations, that this is a one-time flow. Others argue that the private capital flow has been due to the absence of alternative opportunities in the Northern Hemisphere. The United States is just recovering over the last year and a half, and Europe and Japan are still slow. Some say that Latin America has appeal now, because of the recession in the North. But, whatever the truth, growth in Latin America now clearly depends on private capital flows.

On the other side of the equation, I might add that while private capital flows have been important, a large portion of these private flows are now going into long term engagements, not just in the stock market and highly liquid engagements that can be removed rapidly. When we look at 1993's $54.6 billion capital inflow to Latin America, it is estimated that approximately $37.5 billion was net long term transfers, which is a six-fold increase over 1989. So the people who have been sending capital to Latin America have been confident and moving with a greater deal of assurance. I should point out that even in short term or liquid capital flows, such as stock market investment, there has been amazing resilience.

If you look at the case of the Mexican stock market, for example, the performance over this last year was remarkably stable, even though it was one of the most tumultuous years in Mexico since the Mexican Revolution of 1910. There were two major political assassinations and an insurrection and the Mexican stock exchange index had a slight dip after each one, but also a recovery after each dip. After the Chiapas uprising, there was a dip that lasted maybe a month or so, and after the assassination of presidential candidate Colosio, there was a dip that lasted about a month, and again after the assassination of Ruiz Massieu, there was a dip that lasted about two to two and a half months. But again, the recovery in each case is a display of amazing resilience in a medium of exchange where money can be removed easily.

The same thing might be said in the case of Venezuela, by the way, which is the country that appears to have the most difficult circumstances at the moment. The Venezuelan stock exchange index is not that much below its earlier peak, before recent difficulties.

But let's look back at a scary scenario, the early 1980s. Given today's external environment, is it possible that such a scenario could reoccur today? During the 1980s, many Latin governments were running fiscal deficits, and this was fueling inflation, which consequently generated capital flight, unemployment, and the inability of the government to meet social needs.

At the same time, these governments were hit by external shocks. The big external shocks were, of course, the oil price run-up after the fall of the Shah, economic recession in the U.S. and Europe, and the rise of interest rates. These shocks produced the default on debts by Mexico in 1982, and the debt crisis led to the so-called "lost decade" in Latin America. This was a decade in which GDP was reduced from 1980 to 1990 by 0.9 percent, and, because of the population increase, per capita GDP dropped by 1.2 percent. In other words, from 1980 to 1990, people were living worse in Latin America and not improving their status as they were in other areas. So the question we should ask is whether these conditions could repeat themselves today in Latin America?

First of all, looking at the internal economic conditions of the Latin states, in terms of the fiscal situation, we find that many are no longer running deficits. Paradoxically, many of the countries in the underdeveloped world are now finding it easier to run fiscal surpluses or balanced budgets than we are in our country. One of the speakers was saying last night that, paradoxically, in the developing world, they punish agriculture, and in the developed world we subsidize agriculture. By the same token, in the underdeveloped world they are having better luck in maintaining fiscal discipline than we are in the United States. But today we see that Argentina, Chile, and Mexico are all in fiscal surplus. They are all running budgets surpluses this year, and deficits are predicted to shrink below two percent of GDP in a number of major countries, such as Colombia, Peru and Brazil. This is very good news. Only Venezuela, among the major players, will have a fiscal deficit that will approach four percent of GDP. So it is a much better situation in terms of fiscal discipline in the individual Latin states than in the 1980s.

On the monetary side, countries such as Peru, Argentina, Mexico, and even Brazil, for practical purposes, have stable currencies. Fiscal and monetary stability are reinforcing one another.

External influences are also different than they were in the 1980s. The slowness in recovery, and the measures taken by Europe and Japan and the United States to reduce our deficits, have forced international real interest rates down. They are about two percent below the average in the 1980s, at this point in time. So, the Latins will not have to face the problem of a big run-up of interest rates, at least in the immediate future. Inflation in the industrialized countries is also likely to remain low in the next few years. In some sense, that is the bad news, because recovery has not proceeded as fast as we would like in Europe or Japan. But the fact is, inflation is low and therefore the prices that the Latins have to pay for this mass of imports they are receiving will also remain relatively low. The surge in capital flows to the creditworthy countries is likely to continue. Again, because of the slowness of recovery in Europe and Japan, Latin America compares favorably to the rest of the world as a place to send capital. Of course, investor confidence could always be shaken by untoward events, but things don't look terribly bad right now. World trade is likely to continue to grow, especially with the approval of NAFTA and of the Uruguay Round of the GATT.

We are going to come out of the Miami Summit with progress towards hemispheric free trade. And that is good news. Also, real commodity prices are likely to remain stable—they are not likely to go down. There have been some supply cutbacks, and recovery, although more moderate than we would like, has occurred in the United States and is going to occur in Europe and Japan. All in all, I would say all signals are against a 1980s crisis repeating itself in the near term. Fiscal and monetary discipline is good and the external environment looks good.

Internally, within each of the Latin states, it becomes a little more complicated. I just noticed some interesting figures last night in a report from our friend Victor Garcia Laredo's project, the Columbus Group, which is an excellent organization of Latin American businessmen. The report which they had commissioned and was done by Hernan Buchi points out that Latin America has still not recovered from that lost decade of the 1980s. Only in Chile and Colombia have per capita income levels increased significantly over 1980. In other words, with the exception of Chile and Colombia, per capita income remains stable or has gone down. In spite of recent progress, Mexico, Argentina and Brazil have per capita income levels similar to or slightly lower than in 1980, and the remaining economies, including Peru, have income levels considerably below those during the lost decade of the 1980s. The same holds true for real salaries and purchasing power. So what we have is a situation in which the Latin countries are trading more, but the welfare of the average citizen has still not gone up that much. And what the Columbus Group points out in their study is that the only way to solve this problem is through sustained growth. According to Buchi's conclusions, the only country in Latin America on a firm path of sustained growth right now is Chile. The others are just in an incipient recovery, they have their macroeconomic stability, they made their structural adjustments, but they have not just yet reached the stage in which we can say they are on a path of sustained growth. The standard of living is not as high as it was in many of the countries. That is still a major problem.

Also, we should point out that the process of economic adjustment generates strains; there is no question about this. For example, the medium and small manufacturers and merchants are stung by the loss of protection and by the rise of domestic interest rates that takes place during these reforms. Part of this rise of domestic interests rates is occasioned by the need to sterilize the large foreign capital inflows that take place, which means that a small or medium manufacturer or merchant has to pay very high interest rates. Some of you may have seen the op-ed piece in the *Wall Street Journal* a few weeks ago by Jacques Rogozinski, who is with the Banobras Bank in Mexico. He talked about the real problem of small and medium manufacturers. This becomes a social, in addition to an economic problem, because these are the people who create the most jobs. Rogozinksy was suggesting that these people have to pay the outrageous local interest rates because they cannot go to foreign banks and get loans at the favorable interest rates that they should. More of them need to bundle their loans and to go into joint purchasing arrangements to make it easier for them to grow. But medium and small manufacturers and merchants are part of the protectionist forces in Latin America and they are suffering and their suffering also impacts job creation.

People who farm in rural areas are often hurt by trade openings. In Mexico, due to NAFTA, there will be an agricultural free market in 15 years. That is good news for American farmers, but it is difficult news for farmers in Mexico who raise corn, who will have to find jobs in the city. And there are lots of them. Up to a few years ago, there were 20 million Mexicans who had no cash income. They were subsistence farmers. They are going to be faced with a necessity to move off the land, and that generates dislocation, difficulty and protest. There are also the urban poor who suffer from the absence of job creation in small and medium size firms. In addition, the funding for some welfare programs has dried up due to budget stringencies. The good news, as we know, is the fiscal discipline that these countries have developed. The bad news is that some "peace" payments to the poor will go down.

These things generate protest. They have to be lived through and overcome to achieve the next stage of economic growth, which will generate job creation. Jobs will take care of these people. Yesterday you heard Congressman Lee Hamilton talk about the need for trade adjustment assistance in the United States. He said that while the opening of trade will create greater gains for our overall economy, there are people who do lose their jobs, and to handle that politically we have to have some kind of trade adjustment assistance to these people. That same argument, of course, can be made in Latin America.

But what Hernan Buchi reminds us is that one dollar directed towards investment will be much more fruitful than one dollar directed toward relief and welfare. In other words, an investment will create multiple jobs in the future, while relief payments only handle the problem of that moment. This is a question of a delicate political balance. One has to see what a populace can tolerate. But clearly, complaints are going to be heard from people whose per capita income has remained stable or has gone down. That can be met either by relief or by banking on investment to create jobs. Those of us who watched the U.S. election results in the last month know that in the United States, too, earnings for middle class and lower class workers have remained stable for about ten years, and this has generated political resentment. Governments in Latin America likewise have to be aware that their own longevity in office may depend to some extent on measures to relieve the dislocations occasioned by adjustment and by the overhang recession of the 1980s.

Another factor, which I will conclude with, is the question of the Latin military. In the past, the Latin military has represented mainly elite elements. In recent years they have come more from the lower middle classes and lower classes. They have more empathy for the suffering of the people of those segments. Those of you who followed the developments in Venezuela, particularly in 1992, know how junior officers there formed the group called the Bolivarian and identified with the adjustment difficulties of the poorer elements. This is a problem.

This phenomenon has come at a time when the Latin militaries have lost a real sense of their mission. During the Cold War, of course, the mission of fighting guerrillas had a larger meaning within world politics. That mission in many countries is gone. The mission of the moment, fighting narcotrafficking, is a very controversial one. Many countries don't want their military involved, because it would open it up to corruption. So the narco mission is difficult. One thing that has provoked a lot of enthusiasm is the idea of peacekeeping. I just came back last week from Camp Santiago, Puerto Rico, where we held a peacekeeping exercise involving the armed forces of Honduras, Guatemala, and El Salvador simulating a division of forces operating in a fictional country and delivering humanitarian assistance. Senior military officials from many of the Latin countries who observed the exercise were very much enthused. This gave them an idea of a mission which is useful in the world. It is a mission that takes them out of their countries, and it is something that is of great interest to them. But those who have not gone on peacekeeping missions, those that have remained in the countries, think a little too much about the difficulties for the poorer elements occasioned by adjustment.

In sum, we can say that in terms of basic economics, fiscal discipline has improved very much in Latin America. Monetary discipline has improved. Dependency between the Latin American countries is deepening as there is greater trade among them. There is greater trade between north and south, with the United States and Canada, which reduces possible political frictions. Adjustment processes are difficult, but the governments are making progress.

Economic Integration: International Perspectives from the Media (I)

DAVID ASMAN

I don't mean to start off with an argument, but it should be mentioned that in Argentina they didn't do the right things because they had an enlightened president; they did them because after two years of bad policies, they faced hyper-inflation and were lucky enough to have an economic minister who knew what to do. I think our Argentine friends might have something to say about that as well.

I am going to be a bit contrarian, because I live and work in New York City where notions of economic liberalism haven't really caught on yet. There is a lot of stuff in *Forbes* and of course in the *Globe and Mail* and the editorial pages of the *Wall Street Journal* which supports the views we all agree on, or that I assume most of us agree on, as regards what works and what doesn't. But the press out there—by the press I mean the vast majority led by the *New York Times*, the *Washington Post*, the various wire services, Reuters and AP—didn't catch on to what was happening in the world, particularly in the emerging markets and more particularly in Latin America, in terms of economic rationalization and the move away from mercantilist and socialist economies. They lost out on that, and now they have woken up to the fact that a lot of these economies—sometimes because of crises, as in Argentina, sometimes because of genuinely en-

David Asman is Senior Editor, the *Wall Street Journal*, and edits the "Americas" column.

lightened leadership as in Mexico and Chile—are moving away from controlled economies. They turned around and suddenly they saw this happening. And after trying to figure it out and deciding whether they should support it, they have come down clearly on the side of pooh-poohing it.

I brought a couple of examples of that with me. The most recent one is from yesterday's Associated Press. The dateline is, Lima, Peru. I'll just read the first three paragraphs:

"The driver of the van that hit 82-year-old Maria Alverto, did stop. But rather than help her, he threw her into the Rhiemarack River, where the injured woman drowned. Aside from the 20-year-old driver's cruelty, the case was newsworthy because he was driving a cumby, the local name for the 30,000 small vans that serve as buses in Lima," (if anyone has read Hernando De Soto, you know about these).

"Although the cumbies have solved what was a transportation crisis in Lima, critics see them as symbolic of the Peruvian government's frantic rush to free market reforms and of the chaos of daily life in the South American capital." And here is a quote from a political analyst. "They opened the market, solved the transportation problem, created a good business and made a big traffic jam."

That is typical of the kind of remarks that are made in the established media about what is happening in Latin America. We have mentioned Chile several times here today, as an example that everybody agrees is positive, not only for the interests of Latin America business and U.S. businesses that deal with them, but indeed for the people at large. Well, if you were to read the *New York Times* religiously, you would note that on September 7 of this year Nathaniel Nash had a piece datelined from Chile, entitled "Latin Economic Speedup Leaves Poor in the Dust." The subtitle is "A Boom, for the Few." This piece quotes a number of people, poor people. Nathaniel, who is a very good journalist, clearly was given guidance by his editors in New York. You can get a sense of those stories generated by the journalist and those generated from the home office. You can just hear the editors in New York calling down to Nathan, who knows better than to write some of the stuff that was written in here, and saying, "Look, all these free market nabobs have been talking about

Chile as the prime example of where the free market really works. Why don't you go down, go down to the shanty towns, get some complaints from the poor people, then go to the World Bank and the IMF and get the testimony from some of the old diehard socialist economists there who recognize that this free market experiment is doomed to failure? Then come up with a brief analysis of the whole thing," which is exactly what the article is.

It starts out with these personal perspectives from poor people who are suffering—poor people suffer everywhere. Of course it doesn't say how badly they were suffering 20 years ago, but you know right now their life is pretty tough, as anybody who is familiar with shanty towns in Latin America knows. So he collect the complaints, and then he gets the prerequisite quotes like this one from an economist and specialist on social reform at the Inter-American Development Bank—one of those wonderful institutions that one hopes Newt Gingrich will know what to do with. Listen to this quote, specifically about Chile: "The resumption of economic growth has been bought at a very high social price, which includes poverty, increased unemployment and income inequality, and this is leading to social problems." So in other words, economic growth has increased unemployment, unemployment has increased poverty, and poverty has increased income disparity. Well, the last of those points may be somewhat true. There are so many more rich people than there are poor people that perhaps, statistically speaking, that is true. But this doesn't mean that poor people are worse off not than they were before.

The point is, the media are taking off after this whole concept of economic liberalism. Included in that, although they're on the run somewhat because of the success of NAFTA and GATT, is economic integration. It has not been taken off the agenda of these editors who are opposed to the process, nor has it been completely resolved within some of the international institutions. Currently, Mexico is perhaps the prime example of a Latin American country that is ravaged by the success of free economic polices. There are articles with their prerequisite statistics and quotes about how American investment has increased, how inflation has decreased, how the capital markets have been taking off and so forth. But then they invariably focus on the poor people and how their lives are much worse now under "neo-liberalism," which is a derogatory catch-all phrase said with a sneer. (Fidel Castro as far as I can tell was the first person who used this word to refer to free market changes.)

Indeed, it has now become fashionable among the journalistic set to sandbag all free-market economic changes. *Newsweek*'s foreign editor, Michael Elliott, in talking about Colosio's assassination and what might have led to it, says, "Economic reform is not cost free, it does not fill empty shelves. It turns societies upside down. In its first stages, it opens the door to sleaze, graft and corruption." He says it as if these "costs" did not exist under statist governments, or mercantilist ones. "It can, and in Mexico it surely did, widen the gap between the poor and the rich." Again, income disparity is always invoked. Here's the *New York Times*, Tim Golden: "What is at stake in Chiapas is no longer just Chiapas or even Mexico, but perhaps even the Free Trade Agreement and the whole neo-liberal project in Latin America." He was wrong on that; that came out right before the NAFTA vote. Anthony De Palma, Tim's assistant or cohort in Mexico, says he "lamented the choice of Ernesto Zedillo after Colosio was killed." He suggested that Mr. Zedillo does not understand "that Mexico has too many millionaires and too many poor people to continue without a clash." Again, the concept of income disparity.

What has to be taken into consideration, even by some people in this panel, in this group who were lamenting some of the aspects of economic reforms, is that there are a variety of different economic reforms out there, all of which have been labeled free market. You have to distinguish between those that work and those that don't, or those that focus just on the elite, as the reforms in Venezuela did in 1988, '89, '90, when Carlos Andres Perez came in. They did not lead to a broadening of the economic base at all. In addition, of course, they were dramatically unpopular, because people saw nothing but rich people getting a lot richer by cornering markets. They didn't see an increase in economic opportunity for themselves. Economic reforms in which there has been economic opportunity available at all levels of the economic strata—from the lowest to the mid to the upper—as happened in Mexico until two years ago when they began to take the IMF's bad advice have been much more successful. Other countries that have focused on the IMF book-balancing solutions as opposed to real entrepreneurial solutions have had political problems.

We have talked about the scandals in Argentina and Brazil and elsewhere. Practically all politicians are corrupt, or at least susceptible to charges of corruption. The charges against Menem, by the way, were close to leading to his downfall right before the spring of 1991 when Cavallo came in. He had only a 20 per cent approval rating that spring. The charges against President Menem's wife and in-laws concerning money laundering and possible dealings with BCCI and other drug laundering institutions had reached a crisis point, and he was on the way out. Menem was on the same road Collor was on. As soon as the economy turned around, as soon as Cavallo came in with his monetary program and his supply-side tax initiatives and regulatory initiatives, Menem's problems went off the front page, back to the back pages, as anybody from Argentina knows.

The same happened to Salinas. Salinas came into power when inflation was 150 percent, when the economic crisis had reached a crescendo, and in a fraudulent election. I think he actually won the election, but it was riddled with fraud, and his popularity was absolutely zilch, until the economy began to turn around. That really changed the whole political perspective. Incidentally, two years ago, when Mexico began to slow its economic program and take the advice of the IMF folks who were worried about it growing too fast in an overheated economy, Salinas's popularity plummeted. Interest rates didn't rise coincidentally; they rose as a part of government strategy to try to slow economic growth. When that happened, Salinas's popularity began to dive, dramatically, and he found himself in a horse race. Until, of course, the Mexican public, helped by a lot of government propaganda and the pumping of the money supply, realized the alternatives were even worse. The alternative was a return to the old socialist ways.

So we have to ask ourselves again, why—despite all of our awareness of what works and what doesn't work, both in economic policy and political policies—why are the media engaged in the current campaign to undermine good social and economic development? The answer is that their livelihood depends on it. The old elite who used to control the money and the ideas concerning developmental economics—ECLA, the Inter-American Development Bank, the IMF, and the other world institutions—these people are now middle-class bureaucrats who have become very accustomed to their six-figure, tax-free salaries. Their livelihood depends on the continued impression that Latin America cannot survive on the basis of the strength and the entrepreneurship of the people. It needs these development banks and it needs either social welfare programs or business welfare programs in order to survive. And they have their friends in the media who they push all the time. They become very friendly with the media. They call you up, take you out to lunch, protest dramatically when you pull out your own American Express Corporate card, and you realize that perhaps not all journalists protest as loudly as the *Wall Street Journal* does, or is able to. That is not to say reporters are bribed to write stories they do not believe in. But then again, the pressure and the influence and the power of these institutions cannot be under-estimated. They have been pushing their buddies in the media to follow the line that the poor are getting poorer, the rich are getting richer, and that what is needed is more of the old redistributionist type of economic policies. Lest we forget, the 1950s, '60s and even part of the '70s were very positive times for Latin America. There was growth, there was tremendous interest on the part of U.S. and European businesses, perhaps now replaced by Asian businesses. That's precisely the point at which the lobbyists for international bu-reaucracies, for international financial institutions not related to the market place but related to government bureaucrats began their strongest push for influence in Latin America. And they succeeded in implementing policies that inhibited private sector competition and increased the role of the state. It is absolutely true, that with the de-mise of the Soviet Union, socialist ideas have lost much of their driv-ing force. However, the battle continues. Those people who believe in socialist and redistributionist ideas still exist. They still believe in sta-tist solutions, and they are still racked with liberal guilt and all the other psychological problems that cause them to defend policies that are not supported by evidence.

So, the battle is goes on, even though we have won NAFTA and GATT, and we are probably going to win Chile's integration. To quote Tom Bray, a former editorialist for the *Wall Street Journal.*

who is now the editorial page editor of the *Detroit News,* after the election a few weeks ago, he said: "And now the institutions." Meaning, now we have to deal with the media. Now we have to deal with the universities. Now we have to deal with the international bureaucracies and the private foundations, all of whom have not yet recognized the things we have recognized.

Economic Integration: International Perspectives from the Media (II)

HOWARD BANKS

I'll start with a quote. "Free trade is one of the greatest blessings which a government can confer on a people. But it is in almost every case and every country unpopular. People prefer to think of their pressure groups and their problems, which are all on the other side of the coin." Now that quote comes from, as near as I can get, 1835, from Thomas Babington, a Whig politician in England. Nothing has changed. Trade is the nearest thing to what a wise old editor I worked for at one time called "a room emptier." It is boring. Nobody cares. Nobody wants to know.

The only way you get trade in the newspapers is to make it dramatic. You have to make it a conflict between A and B. It usually works out that the little guys, the people who feel oppressed by whatever is going on, are the ones that scream loudest and in the most organized fashion. They are the easiest ones to listen to and so it is their views that get more coverage. By the nature of things—all the way since Babington, who became Lord Macaulay—they tend to be the trendy lefties, socialist-leaning activists. So there we are, left with it. Take as an example, NAFTA a debacle for the press. The press was totally on the wrong side of the issue for 90 percent of the time and most of the press were taken by surprised by the outcome, I would guess. Also, the press failed to understand the importance of

Howard Banks is Washington Bureau Chief of *Forbes*.

delinking MFN as it affected China, believing what the IMF and the World Bank types say. They *believe* that stuff. And it is easier to believe the anti-free trade case, because you can't prove very easily the numbers on the pro-free trade side of the case, because the pro-trade case is diffuse. The beneficiaries of free trade are all of us.

People look at me as though I am barmy when I recite the numbers concerning the cost of protection. Example: Textile protection in the United States benefits two percent of the working population in the textile and apparel business, including retailing. Yet it accounts for 83 percent of the net cost of U.S. trade protection. These are not my numbers; they are from the National Bureau of Economic Research. This adds an estimated $700 per year to the clothing bill of every family of four in the United States. And thanks to a very clever one word change in GATT—it's called the Fruit of the Loom Amendment—that cost over the next four years will rise to $900 per family per year. Thanks to GATT. Praise be for free trade and all that.

Here is a splendid and theoretically true idea that is politically impossible. Just open your borders up totally to trade and you will be better off. It is, of course, unprovable and I doubt that it will ever happen. Take a look at a micro example, Boeing versus Airbus. Airbus was started as a make-work job protection program in Europe and it has so far cost the Europeans $12 billion. That's an estimate I use, but it is no more than a guess because the numbers are all buried in government guarantees and loans and fiddles and lies. Boeing, even now that the U.S.'s leading exporting company, has fought government subsidies for Airbus like mad. Eventually Boeing got a deal, through GATT, to limit them. Incidentally, the deal achieved the most important thing for Boeing, which is price discipline. Airbus no longer gives away airplanes. The Europeans no longer so blatantly give away landing rights to countries that buy Airbuses. But note: Even mighty Boeing could not stand back and say it was in the greater glory of the United States (in terms of benefit to travelers) to allow free entry, at any level of subsidy, for these quite splendidly advanced Airbus airplanes. Airbus, because it doesn't worry much about profits, has been ahead in every technical move there has been. For the airlines, this has been an amazingly good thing. But even Boeing demanded some protection against Airbus.

I will conclude with four short observations. I was brought up by a father who was an English liberal with a capital L. Not an American liberal. One of the things that I remember hearing from an early age is that "trade follows the flag." One of the things that really bothers me right now in the American attitude is increasingly inward-looking. The U.S. has won the war it began at Bretton Woods. The underlying theme of all that followed Bretton Woods was to prevent yet more European wars, to defeat the Communists, all that. And to avoid repeating the disasters that followed World War I right through to 1945. That was a modern economic dark age really. It is worth remembering (as Treasury Undersecretary Lawrence H. Summers has pointed out) that global economic trade and cross-border investment flows, expressed as percentages of world GDP, are only now just about back to where they were before the first World War.

The success of the last 50 years has occurred because the U.S. was rich enough and somehow wise enough to be generous, always to be the one who gave, always to be the one who had a little bit of money to help these things along. That is no longer the case. The willingness to lead in this way seems to me to be declining, and that augurs ill for the future growth in world trade at a time when we ought to be looking to the world to grow like crazy. We should be in for 30 years of world growth, assuming we can avoid some stupid war, assuming the Chinese do not go in for adventurism in southeast Asia, assuming the Islamic fundamentalist trend doesn't get out of hand. Somehow the U.S. has to be brought back to being generous, because it is in the best interests of the U.S. Getting that into the newspapers, let me tell you, is practically impossible.

I am also concerned about the move to regional trade blocs. In particular, I'm concerned about any hint that we might move towards bilateral trade deals. If you want to know how bad bilateral deals can be, especially in the multiple, just look at the international airline industry, where fares average 40 percent higher than they do in the U.S. Everything simply ends up at the highest common factor. (I know everybody says the lowest common denominator, but they get it wrong.) Bilaterals end up being protection for the weak, the highest cost, the doziest, the sloppiest. Capacity controls and all those other bad things are part of these aviation trade deals and would no doubt be part of broader bilateral trade agreements. Bilateral deals are immensely dangerous and restrictive.

Another point always to bear in mind, and I don't think I have heard it very much here, is the importance of opening up cross border investment—the most important factor in generating growth in any area.

Finally, I hope the U.S. will stop constantly trying to convert all these other countries into tiny images of the United States system. The most important thing is just to encourage developing countries to grow. Encourage economic development and democracy will follow.

If you look at the poorest countries, the first thing that happens is they get electricity. That supplants elbows with horsepower, through electric motors. This immediately multiplies the productivity of an ordinary human. The next step is they get a bit more protein and carbohydrate than they had before. Look at the way expatriate Chinese billionaires are going back in the Peoples Republic and growing prawn and chickens, using old rice paddies. There is an absolutely fantastic change in the ability of people to work if they are actually fed a bit.

After that, open up these countries' borders to trade. Along the way, you have to allow the rich to become richer, because that way the poor become richer. Income disparity is, however, a subject you can't get right in the newspapers even when it concerns the United States. We've got upward migration in income levels in the United States that is absolutely staggering. But as long as you have everybody in the press saying it isn't, then, unfortunately, nobody much will believe it.

I'll leave you with this thought—my main problem with writing about trade is that even in the respectable press, it is really very hard to get positive, good, accurate stories into the paper. Believe me.

Economic Integration: International Perspectives from the Media (III)

PETER COOK

Canada's Experience with Free Trade: A Media View

Thank you for inviting me. As someone who has followed the FTA and NAFTA debates in Canada, I feel that I may have more history to recount than my colleagues. That is because the big event in Canada, unlike here and in Mexico, was the FTA of 1988. It was something on which an election was fought and a lot of passion spent. It split the country between pro-free trade and anti-free trade camps and it divided us politically. The Conservatives who had negotiated the deal on the pro-side. The Liberals and socialist New Democrats on the anti-side.

By comparison, the NAFTA debate of 1993, though it also coincided with an election, was quiet and unemotional. NAFTA was billed as an improvement on the FTA and largely accepted as such. And there were no sucking sounds to the south for Canadians. Statistics showed us doing less trade with Mexico than with Singapore, though that is changing now.

Six years after 1988 and the free trade election, Canada under the Liberals (they were the antis back then) is officially enthusiastic

Peter Cook is the Economics Editor and a columnist for *The Globe and Mail Report on Business*, Toronto, Canada.

about regional free trade. In fact, very enthusiastic. It is ready to sign free trade deals all over this hemisphere and elsewhere (Israel is the latest choice). It wants NAFTA expanded to include Chile and then others. If you are looking for a parallel with Europe, Canadians are the Belgians of NAFTA. there is no more ardent integrationist than Trade Minister Roy MacLaren. And although he represents the conservative wing of the Liberal party, he has the support of Prime Minister Jean Chretien. Remember this is the party that under John Turner, Mr. Chretien's predecessor, was going to demand a renegotiation of the FTA in the winter of 1988-89 and, when they didn't get it, rip it up page by page.

What happened to change political attitudes? And how much has the public—which, in 1988, voted down the FTA if one considers that the share of the vote taken by the Liberals and New Democrats was greater than the Conservatives—changed its views?

Now I don't want this to get too complicated. But, in the past, the Liberals who have been the natural governing party, the amorphous centrists of Canadian politics, have been both pro-free trade with the United States—that is when it was mooted before, earlier in the century—and the great supporters of GATT and the international trading system. To some extent, in their rethinking of NAFTA, they have grafted multilateralism on to NAFTA. And they have done it in a way that is sensible and sellable in Canada.

We trade overwhelmingly with the United States but—except in a group—we cannot influence its trade policy. At a time when GATT and the WTO faces a lot of criticism in your country, an enlarged NAFTA may be a better bet. And from the Canadian standpoint the larger the better. When the idea of Mexico doing a free trade deal was first suggested, Canada wanted it to be done within NAFTA for defensive reasons. It did not want to be excluded from a hub-and-spoke relationship between Mexico and the United States.

Now defensive Canada has become aggressive Canada. It wants NAFTA expanded to as many nations as want to join and are prepared to accept the obligations of membership. The Liberals, when elected, said they wouldn't sign NAFTA unless it was changed and new arrangements worked out on subsidy and countervail. A working group was established to look into it. And the Liberals were happy to sign. Their change of mind about free trade took place suddenly. But there were several landmark policy conferences at which the party moved, step by step, away from ripping up the FTA to living with it.

That, in turn, reflected public opinion. For three years after 1988, anti-free trade sentiment was strong. In the three years between 1991 and 1994 it has weakened so that it is now confined to the Canadian Labour Congress and their politically weak friends, the New Democrats.

Those two periods coincided with a sharply different economic performance—in the first inflation gave way to recession, in the second deflation gave way to recovery. The connection between what was happening in the real economy and public opinion on free trade is close.

When an economy is uncompetitive, goods are being priced out of international markets, and newspapers are full of pictures of padlocked factory gates, economic policy makers take the blame—unless the blame is deflected by a newly-signed, much-publicized FTA which its critics said would devastate industry and employment. In the late 1980s, Canada went through what the U.S. had gone through earlier. Our high-dollar period coincided with the introduction of the FTA. The Canadian dollar actually peaked at close to 90 cents in November 1991. Because costs were high and the economy uncompetitive, trade policy became the whipping boy for monetary and fiscal policy.

The actual sequence of events was this. Canadian Governments, federal and provincial, kept on stimulating the economy after 1986 when they should have been restraining it. In 1988, a new Bank of Canada Governor set out to reverse this state of affairs and get inflation down to zero (where it now resides).

Because monetary policy was the main instrument used, interest rates rose and the Canadian dollar shot upward in value. This occurred just as the FTA was being phased in and its effect on an inflationary economy where productivity had lagged was extremely damaging. That effect was most serious in sectors that were least competitive. In other words, the kind of firms that got hurt were the kind of firms you would expect to get hurt—whether by a monetary tightening or by free trade. Since we had just fought a high-profile election on free trade and since the ruling conservatives were rapidly making themselves unpopular, free trade took the whole knock.

Obviously, I am not saying that the FTA did not create bankruptcies and dislocation and lost jobs. It is noticeable that it was our manufacturing industry that went into recession first, and this is where the productivity gap has been largest vis-a-vis the United States, because of shorter local production runs.

What happened, in fact, was that the combination of free trade and a tough monetary policy that pitched us into recession made the process of economic adjustment much tougher and, ultimately, much quicker. As a result, the benefits of restructuring and of getting costs down also showed up sooner.

Look at the trade numbers and free trade was actually doing good even when it was most unpopular. For instance, if you take Canadian exports from 1989 to 1992, those going to the United States outperformed those going to the rest of the world in 13 of 16 categories. I am quoting here from the study *Canada's Performance under Free Trade,* by Daniel Schwanen for the C.D. Howe Institute of Toronto. In the same four years, exports of goods liberalized by the FTA to the United States grew by 33 per cent, while the same exports to all other markets went up only 2 per cent. What's more, the biggest difference in came in non-resource value-added products: office and telecommunications equipment, precision instruments, machinery and equipment. Just the kind of products that Canadians, who suffer from an inferiority complex over being resource-rich, want to sell.

The happy ending to this story is that perceptions did change, as recession gave way to recovery, and that recovery was led by exports to the United States. And then with the NAFTA deal and the promise of new markets in Mexico and Latin America, public opinion came around. The main event was once again the turn in the economy and lower interest rates, and a Canadian dollar valued at 70 to 75 cents rather than 85 to 90 cents.

It was that main event that also brought Canadians to a realization that free trade was working quite well. And that in turn produced the political change that I mentioned earlier and the considerable enthusiasm that now exists for still-lower trade barriers and new trade deals.

Next Steps in the Business Community in Shaping and Promoting Economic Integration in the Hemisphere (I)

HARRY L. FREEMAN

The Miami Summit
in the Context of the New Politics

When one writes a paper in late November, just in advance of the most important trade vote in Congress in decades scheduled for December 2, there is an obvious problem. Therefore, this paper assumes a positive GATT vote, by a thin margin. I also seek permission to amend my remarks when the reality of the GATT vote is known.

The Washington trade community, like ancient Gaul, is divided into three parts. Part one is the trade policy community, which is made up largely of very bright, concerned, experienced trade hands who are almost exclusively concerned with policy initiatives, observations on events, opinions on what should happen, and the like. Unfortunately, these people tend not to be active politically in advancing their views and tend to rely on the inherent logic of the situation to bring out a good result.

Part two is a very different set of bright, concerned experienced trade hands whose principal occupation is lobbying for or against a trade measure, usually in its entirety. These people are drawn from the corporate community (usually "pro" trade legislation), organized labor (often "anti" trade legislation), consumer and

---

Harry L. Freeman is President, the Freeman Company.

environmental organizations, and the like. They measure success in "winning" and "losing," not much in between, and envy those exclusively in policy group number one who seem to avoid the trenches.

Part three are largely trade lawyers who are concerned with specific client interests and specific provisions in trade legislation, dumping cases, proceedings before courts, proceedings before the International Trade Commission, and the like.

There are people who have roles in all three communities. I lay claim to belong to the two first groups, i.e., the "thinkers" and the "actors." In the past few months with the vote on the GATT approaching I have been much more on the "acting" side and critical of my colleagues who concern themselves with policy without doing anything to advance it in concrete ways. Thus in the runup to the GATT vote, we were in real trouble but few were actually working to get votes committed on the pro side. My experience in Washington is that for something to happen, people have to get out and work for it.

For those in the policy community solely concerned with Western Hemisphere issues, the truth is that without a positive outcome to the GATT vote, there is precious little to talk about in Miami a week subsequent to the scheduled GATT vote. The policy people also tend to see trade issues detached from other issues and the realpolitik involved. To me, the Miami meeting is primarily a political event, not an economic one. The political considerations are now supreme, the economic consequences may come later. Therefore the trade policy community may be disappointed with a poor Miami result but would have themselves largely to blame if they didn't actively campaign for the GATT vote. The road to Miami is getting 60 U.S. Senators present and voting for a budget waiver on December 2.

Having won a narrow GATT victory is good news but heavily discounted; while it was really close, few believed in their heart of hearts that "good" would lose to "not-good."

What then is the present political equation vis a vis the Miami summit?

1) The President has no authority to negotiate any new trade agreements (save "carryover" areas of unfinished business in the Uruguay Round of GATT, since trade law allows fast track for such "carryover" areas). Hence, the President has a credibility problem at

the outset. Other Western Hemisphere leaders will question among themselves what the chances are for the President to obtain new negotiating authority, having lost that issue in 1994 and with the new political ground in Washington.

2) In providing the critical votes needed in the House and Senate to obtain a majority for GATT, the new Republican leadership, de facto until January 1995, but with real power now, made it crystal clear that

a) future trade policy was primarily a Congressional concern rather than an Administration concern

b) with very clear negotiating instructions going to the Executive,

c) with potentially adverse and intensive Congressional consultations all the way,

d) with a grant of a modified fast track where much less power is ceded from the Congress to the Executive, and

e) with any positive kudos going to both the Executive and the Republicans in Congress.

If any Western Hemisphere (WH) country doesn't like the new more Congressionally oriented U.S. approach to negotiating trade deals in the Hemisphere, the congressional attitude is more likely to be "take it or leave it" rather than seeking common ground. The new politics will also tend to push U.S. demands higher, and favor replication of the NAFTA, clearly the most advantageous U.S. multilateral trade agreement ever negotiated, rather than something watered down from NAFTA rules.

Another political element may be timing. The new Congressional leadership may wish to ratify a new trade deal with the Western Hemisphere only with a Republican in the White House—that means 1997 to optimistic Republicans.

During the negotiations, if any take place in 1995 or 1996, it seems obvious that presidential politics, particularly on the Republican side (but also on the Democratic side if President Clinton is challenged in his primaries) will play a major role. It will not be an easy negotiation. Perot and his allies will be screaming "our factories will all go south" during each day of negotiation.

What, then, is a caring, intelligent, politically savvy Democratic President, like Bill Clinton, to do?

I believe there is a path through the political thickets for the Administration and the new Congress.

It has a few "simple" elements:

1) Consult before the Miami summit with the Congressional leadership and try to achieve a consensus.

2) Announce the general intention of the U.S. to work towards a free trade zone (or agreement) in the WH, over time, perhaps omitting a time deadline.

3) Further announce that the U.S. is not the country to decide, solo, the next steps towards free trade in the WH, i.e., whether that be an expansion of NAFTA, Mercosur-NAFTA negotiations, bilateral deals, a new Trade round in the WH, or whatever. However, it is up to all WH countries; a Senior Ministerial level group ought to be formed, to consult and try to achieve a consensus on how to proceed, terms of reference, i.e., the whole pathway. The Ministerial Group would need a Chair and a very modest secretariat. Perhaps advisory groups, a la APEC, might be formed. It would be scheduled to report its recommendations one year hence . . . towards the end of 1995. This Ministerial Group should be a serious, highest possible level group. If President Salinas does not become head of the WTO, this might be an opportunity for him to chair that group.

4) Meanwhile, in early 1995, the President, in consultation with the Congress, develops and presents legislation which would include a modified fast track, negotiating goals, and the like. This will probably take most of the year to work its way through the congress and no doubt there will be a national debate on trade policy. This will be occurring while the Ministerial Conference does its work on how to approach free trade zone negotiations.

Nevertheless, I think this route is the only route possible in the present political situation. It preserves a bipartisan approach to trade, at least on the surface and perhaps below the surface as well. An adversarial approach would result in no trade legislation, no authority to negotiate trade deals. I also believe that the commencement of negotiations in 1995 without a mandate from the Congress is advisable, i.e., a nonstarter. And, obviously, I believe that our partners in this hemisphere should be part of the process to determining the road map. Of course, the U.S. remains the 800 pound gorilla in the WH but should use that might constructively with the other countries.

Always the optimist I predict that we will conclude major trade negotiations leading to some form of "free trade" in the WH by 1997 or 1998, with the results phased in pretty quickly thereafter. Without wishing to get into the subject further, I believe the WH deal will be the precedent setter for both new negotiations in the WTO and for APEC.

Indeed, if a real free trade deal can be worked out in the WH by 1997 or 1998, it could have a major positive impact on APEC's negotiations. I believe the APEC goal of 2020 is so far beyond anyone's horizon, albeit an accomplishment to get the diverse APEC countries to agree on anything. A really open trade regime in the WH could easily spur APEC to a more aggressive timetable.

Addendum

As with the other paper for this conference, I am writing this on the day of the house vote on GATT and a day or two before the Senate vote. I am assuming the GATT passes easily in the House and by a narrow margin in the Senate.

In addressing the question of the "business community," in general, there is no such thing. There are hundreds of trade associations representing specific industries, i.e., chemical manufacturers, pharmaceuticals, banks, etc. There are multiple industry groups such as the Business Roundtable (BRT), the National Association of Manufacturers. There are also groups primarily dealing with trade issues such as the Emergency Committee for American Trade (ECAT).

For each major trade initiative there has been a special business coalition formed, which is typically a loose federation of existing trade associations. I had the privilege of forming the coalition favoring and securing a broad trade agreement between the U.S. and Canada in 1986-87. I also had the privilege of being executive director of the huge business coalition favoring a strong and broad result to the Uruguay Round of the GATT (MTN Coalition). We dissolved that immediately after the negotiations concluded in December 1993. We contemplated that a new business coalition would be formed with the sole purpose of lobbying the U.S. Congress to secure passage. That did occur and the Alliance for GATT NOW, led by the Business Roundtable, has been doing the job all of 1994.

Involvement in 1994 by the business community in major initiatives that go beyond specific industry issues, such as Western Hemisphere free trade agreement, I argue, needs a special coalition. The challenges are leadership and funding.

With the U.S. Canada FTA, we had little problem. When I led it I was an Executive Vice President of American Express, and I devoted much time to it, as did its then CEO, Jim Robinson. Robinson was also chair of the Business Roundtable trade task force and also chaired the President's Advisory Committee on Trade Policy Negotiations. Those positions gave Robinson and dominant position in trade matters in Washington. Since American Express' policy was to be positive on all open trade issues, rather than just its own issues, there was major leadership in that effort.

The MTN Coalition, formed in 1990, was easy at the start. I had just retired from American Express Company, but Robinson still held all of the positions mentioned above. He was able to secure funding ($2,000,000) for MTN in about 15 minutes' time, assuming a two year life of the coalition with predictable activities. After the two years went by and the finish of the Round was still years off, funds became harder to raise, but it was done. Legitimate, but unanswerable questions were raised, such as "How much more will this cost me, and when will this be over?" The truth was "who knows?" Hence funds became harder to come by.

Then, while GATT was still being negotiated, NAFTA blew into the trade debate with a vengeance after Perot's trashing of it in the presidential debate. The BRT usually takes the lead in forming coalitions and Robinson proceeded to do so. Unfortunately, in early 1993 just after NAFTA coalition was formed, Robinson left American Express and his BRT membership was over. The BRT is limited to sitting CEOs. His successor in the BRT was the chair of Kodak. In a case of very bad luck, he was also a former chair of Kodak within months. The BRT trade chair remained empty for some months. So it was not until late in the battle in 1993 when Larry Bossidy, chair of

Allied Signal, took over the BRT trade task force and the NAFTA coalition. Bossidy was outstanding. Most importantly, we won.

Meanwhile, the MTN limped (financially speaking) through to the end of the round in December, 1993, with some of its workers going on a volunteer unpaid status towards the end.

The new GATT coalition was formed in 1994 by the new BRT trade task force chair, Jerry Junkins, chair of Texas Instruments. The TI Washington office became the lead office and the BRT staffer in charge of trade (Paula Collins) became a major point person. Collins had served her 10 years internship at American Express Company working for it on trade issues all along.

While funding for the new GATT coalition was raised, it was increasingly difficult. When the vote was put off from this past September until a special session in late November, a lot of corporate fatigue set in, both in terms of funding and in terms of lobbying efforts. At the end the preponderance of television advertising was against GATT, not for it. there is also the question of whether ads help either side.

Turning to the Western Hemisphere, ideally the scenario would be the formation of a new trade coalition which becomes the federation of existing associations and companies. I think this will be very difficult. The outlook for negotiations will probably be several years, perhaps closing in 1997 or 1998 at the earliest with Congressional review in 1998 or 199 at the earliest. Unless one company or industry comes up with a respected leader who can raise funds, and run a multiple year coalition while also doing the job as CEO of a major corporation.

Is such a coalition necessary? No, but highly desirable. The U.S. does need a cheerleader function.

Why am I pessimistic about a new Western Hemisphere coalition?

1) No obvious CEO is apparent to me who is both good at this kind of task and will make the time and financial commitment.

2) Corporate fatigue in funding coalitions almost nonstop from 1986.

3) A probable perception of "no need now" by many corporations.

4) The good old days of passing trade legislation easily by wide margins are gone forever; trade is now a populist issue, demagogued readily, and will need increasing effort and money with each new deal. I doubt if Perot, Pat Buchanan, United We Stand, Nader and others will just go away if they lose GATT. A trade deal with poorer countries in this hemisphere is more easily attacked than GATT.

I expect major trade legislation next year in the form of both fast track and negotiating priorities and the corporations and their associations will be weighing in more in parochial issues than advancing the general principle of open trade being in the U.S. national interest.

Next Steps in the Business Community in Shaping and Promoting Economic Integration in the Hemisphere (II)

This is a synthesis of a paper, entitled "Latin America: Sustained Economic Growth," which was prepared by the Columbus Group for the Summit of the Americas.

For those of you who are unfamiliar with it, the Columbus Group was created in the mid-Eighties by a group of Latin American and Latin European businessmen who share an interest in Latin American economic, social and cultural issues. Its members are committed to changing and revitalizing Latin America, so that the region can respond efficiently to the profound changes taking place in the world today.

The Columbus Group is a non-profit organization and is not linked to any political party or movement.

Introduction

Latin America is currently enjoying a moment of great hope. The Summit of the Americas is taking place at a time when all the nations of the region—some more than others—have begun in-depth political, economic and social reforms. They have abandoned

---

Victor Garcia Laredo is Managing Director of the Columbus Groups, a non-profit association of top business executives from Latin America that fosters regional integration and overseas investment in Latin America.

authoritarianism and state-run economies and have moved on to building democratic societies and free market economies. This process has led to new optimism: now there are valid expectations for progress. But at the same time, the process is tiring and often accompanied by impatience. The Summit of the Americas provides an opportunity for the continent to officially commit to democracy and free markets while agreeing on an agenda to make them a reality in long-suffering Latin America.

The Summit is taking place just a few years after Latin America began its "lost decade" caused by the foreign debt crisis. Between 1980 and 1990 the region's economic growth was only 0.9 percent, meaning a 1.2 percent drop in the per capita GDP. The debt crisis shook the entire region, affecting Mexico, Central America and the Southern Cone at different times and with differing intensities. The decline in economic activity caused a notable increase in unemployment, a drop in real salaries and many bankruptcies.

The economic turmoil at the beginning of the Eighties made some people think that we were on the brink of another Great Depression, that financial upheaval would bring on more political authoritarianism and strengthen the government's hold on the economy. In the end, the results were exactly the opposite. For a time it seemed the debt crisis and the crumbling capital markets would block any possibility of private initiative-based development, and that ensuing social costs would indefinitely postpone democracy's arrival on the continent.

But history often takes a strange course. The "lost decade" proved to be a great lesson. Latin America realized that the root of the problem lay in previous decades of bloated government; in the belief that legitimate expectations of well-being could be met by state intervention in the markets; and in the consequent disdain for private initiative. This bitter lesson of crisis led stability and structural reforms, which began in country after country throughout the 1980s and the early 1990s. These reforms have planted the seeds of progress and will prove that, in the long run, the decade of the 1980s, far from being lost, was enormously fruitful.

The progress of these reforms has been greeted with understandable optimism in the Americas and in the world. If the reforms stay on course, in ten more years Latin America may be the next Southeast Asia. But the enthusiastic applause generally ignores the fact that it will be awhile before the reforms bear fruit. Latin America continues to be burdened by the heavy crisis it inherited.

The reforms are attempting to restart sustained growth, creating jobs and overcoming poverty. But in vast areas of the region, this growth has not yet arrived, or if it has arrived, it has not lasted long enough to reduce poverty. The Chiapas of the past and of the future show that the economic issue has yet to be solved, that we do not yet have growth and that efforts must be increased.

Reform Program

Let me describe briefly the three phases of the reform process, as they are taking place in our countries:

- In the initial stage, the emphasis is on stability and controlling inflation through appropriate changes to the fiscal, monetary and exchange policies. During this phase efforts are made to reestablish access to foreign credit by balancing foreign accounts and restructuring or reducing foreign debt.

- The second stage involves structural reforms, like opening up trade and the financial sector to foreign investors, allowing prices to be set by the market, encouraging capital goods imports, freeing up productivity factors and reducing government size and spending.

- The third stage is one of sustained growth which demands a notable increase in investment and both private and public savings, as well as careful management of the macroeconomic policy to maintain positive conditions for growth.

The different Latin American economies show varying degrees of progress on these reforms. Some—like Brazil, Ecuador, Uruguay and Venezuela—are still in the initial stage. their most immediate need is to obtain or consolidate economic stability that will permit later growth. Others—like Argentina, Bolivia, Chile, Colombia, Mexico, Peru and a number of Central American economies—are making headway in the second stage and are no longer affected by big swings on a macroeconomic level. Some have made notable progress in controlling inflation. Argentina, Bolivia and Mexico, which all have suffered from soaring inflation in the past, now boast single digit rates. Chile, Colombia and Peru are slowly advancing in the same direction.

Chile along appears well rooted in the third stage, that of sustained growth. With an estimated fixed investment rate of 27 percent of the GDP and an estimated national savings rate of 25 percent of the GDP in 1994, Chile is the only country in the region that seems to be enjoying a true economic takeoff. By all appearances Argentina, Colombia, Mexico and Peru are the leading candidates to follow in Chile's footsteps of success.

I want to point out that many of today's problems, like unemployment, society's impatience with the apparent lack of progress, lagging exchange rates and high interest rates are partly a result of prior conditions, but are also due to the difficulties inherent in coordinating and synchronizing difference reform programs.

Important Objectives

In order to achieve accelerated growth, reforms must be emphasized and carried out in depth. In our opinion, arduous tasks remain ahead, but as the sensation of crisis wanes it is likely that the desire to continue with the reform process will decline. Therefore, it is crucial to have a continental commitment and international cooperation for the agenda we propose. The agenda should include the following principal objectives: increasingly opening the economy through economic integration; continuing privatization; increasing competitiveness; achieving great indices of human development and overcoming new dangers arising from protectionism, the desire for redistribution of wealth and radical ecological movements.

Economic Integration

The opening of economies, trade, finances, telecommunications and technology is the key to Latin America growth. It is clear that Latin America—with only nine percent of the world's GDP and combined exports representing only 3.5 percent of total world exports—can only achieve sustained growth if it can interest the vital North American, European and Asian markets. The success of "outward" growth strategies is so overwhelmingly superior to our traditional "inward" growth that no further debate the essential opening of our economies.

Real international integration, including free trade as a medium-range objective, is required for further opening of the economy. Subsidies for exports and tax benefits for domestic production must also be eliminated; health and hygiene standards must be made uniform throughout the region; and the practice of exchange controls and tax restrictions on transferring capital must be ended. An open economy also means equal treatment for local and foreign investors, canceling double taxation agreements and implementing reasonable immigration procedures Physical integration must be fostered by eliminating excessive border controls, enabling joint use of road and port infrastructure and encouraging connection between national power and information systems.

Each country in the region, in keeping with its particular history and current situation, has chosen its own path to an open economy. Some have chosen a unilateral path, confident that the strength of their deeds and international pressure via the GATT will eventually bring down other countries' protective barriers. Others have opted for sub-regional trade agreements—on a Latin American level we have Mercosur, the Andean Pact, the Central American Common Market and others. Free trade agreements with the United States and Canada—of which NAFTA is the most important—have also been put into effect. All of these paths should be considered initial steps toward a Pan American Free Trade Agreement.

Continuing Privatization

Privatization is crucial in our economies, because it assures that the private sector has the necessary incentive, management and resources to take advantage of new opportunities and increased efficiency that open markets make possible. It also gives private initiative a chance to participate in investment opportunities like mining, energy supply and distribution, telecommunications, infrastructure and transportation—areas that tend to be big producers and prone to production bottlenecks, which can't be efficiently developed by the public sector due to the lack of adequate resources and incentives.

Privatization also allows the government to unload unprofitable companies or sell the money-making ones and concentrate its resources on developing human resources and fighting poverty, areas in which its efforts are essential. It also leads to a wider distribution of property and the accompanying economic political and commercial benefits. This is especially valid if the procedures lead to the creation of "new capitalists."

Recently several Latin American countries have made significant progress in selling public companies to the private sector. Argentina, especially, has made great strides in privatization, as have Brazil, Chile, Mexico and Peru, to a lesser degree.

Human Development

One of the issues that still causes Latin Americans a great deal of pain is that the region continues to show low human development indices. For example, an estimate 18 percent of the region's people live in poverty. Although these figures are used for political purposes, and therefore are not always trustworthy, the truth is that unfulfilled needs continue to be an enormous problem. The statistics for infant mortality, nutrition, life expectancy, literacy and education are quite unacceptable. In terms of infant mortality rates, only Uruguay, Chile, Costa Rica and Cuba have acceptable rates. Rectifying these deficiencies is an overwhelming task and, being such a sensitive matter which lends itself easily to demagoguery, should only be dealt with professionals on a technical basis.

As I have just mentioned, the main danger is in interpreting the poverty figures as being caused by the reforms. The reforms are still too new to be held responsible for these problems. The figures reflect the dramatic inheritance from decades of slow or non-existent growth and disjointed social policies. The solution can be found in strengthening growth and improving social programs.

Eradicating poverty requires decentralizing and privatizing social security, government housing, education and health. The government should limit itself to regulating and subsidizing the demand for these services for the poor sectors of society. The social security model used by Argentina, Chile, Colombia and Peru is an example of this. The principles it is based on can easily be extended to other social areas.

Every country should choose its own path according to its particular situation, but human development is a fertile area for international cooperation. Governmental agencies with international assistance and multilateral organizations such as the World Bank and the Inter-American Development Bank should be the first to be involved.

New Dangers

I want to emphasize that new issues and dangers can arise from the flow of events and politics. Or rather, old problems take on new forms and can become powerful obstacles to growth.

The principal source of new dangers is veiled protectionism, disguised as labor rights or ecological protection. The danger is serious because it attacks the heart of our strategy: our ability to compete advantageously in an integrated world.

Labor protectionism maintains that anything produced at low labor costs is unfair competition because workers rights are supposedly abused. If such abuse exists, it should be brought to the attention of the respective national and international bodies that deal with this problem. But to suppose that free trade should be based on equal costs is to ignore the principle of comparative advantages. It is perfectly natural that labor costs are lower in poorer countries, just as their cost of capital is higher than in richer countries. As mentioned, job creation is one of the most effective mechanisms there is to fight poverty and labor protectionism is one of its principal enemies.

The situation is similar to "ecological dumping," or the principle of competitive products manufactured under lax environmental standards and exported to industrialized economies Environmental standards are not similar in all countries, as each individual country must make its own decisions involving the proper balance between economic growth and the conservation of its own environment.

Analysis and cooperation, including financial assistance to solve this problems would be valuable and very effective. Once again, specialized organizations should play an important role in this process.

Conclusions

As I mentioned earlier, sustained growth is fundamental if the problems inherent to the region's poverty are to be solved. Development is the best passport for personal advancement: jobs that allow men to progress thanks to their own efforts and not to the patronage of third parties.

We also know that sustained growth is indispensable if we want to consolidate the democratic process, halt corruption and begin protecting our environment.

We should not let a day go by without taking a step forward to make possible new endeavors. We must be brave and break vicious prejudices. It has been proven over and over again that many rules which supposedly protect workers, in reality only cause unemployment and stagnation. Nonetheless, much of the region has yet to enact labor reform legislation. It is true that governments need much of resources, but it is also true that they spend enormous amounts in useless tasks, unproductive bureaucracy, or sectors that are not the neediest. many of the countries have made progress, but much remains to be done. The job will be finished only when the tax burden levied on producers is lightened, allowing them to grow a bit more every day.

Historic responsibility rests on all of us, the private sector, governments and international organization for cooperation.

Private initiative has the starring role in this new model of Latin American development. Businessmen are the ones who must believe in the possibilities this new model offers, and place their bets on a Latin American takeoff. They are the ones who should create new initiatives, update their companies, invest in productive capital, infrastructure and labor resources, encourage savings that will finance these investments, gain new markets in the region and abroad, increase employment and salaries, and pay taxes to finance governments. Business organizations should lobby for goo economic policies, and support free market reforms that are in the best interests of the companies and the country.

The government of the United States has a fundamental role to play here and should make an unfailing public commitment to do its best to expand NAFTA according to objective criteria.

It should be a real model of free trade and a champion of free trade in the world. It should aid the integration of the Americas in other areas mentioned, including: energy, information, infrastructure, finance and population. It should strengthen international organizations that give financial assistance. This will support the reform process and neutralize possible macroeconomic destabilizing pressures. The government of the United States should, above all, follow a stable and predictable course in its international policies concerning Latin America, as well as in its economic policies, which have always had deep repercussions on the entire continent, and could affect the possibility of achieving several decades of sustained economic growth.

All this will mean better opportunities for all the countries of the Americas to achieve a better standard of living and will increase our possibilities of working together to achieve this goal.

Next Steps in the Business Community in Shaping and Promoting Economic Integration in the Hemisphere (III)

TIMOTHY PAGE

Thanks to both the Hudson and Fraser Institutes for the opportunity to provide a Canadian business perspective to these proceedings. Many of the remarks that have been made at the conference thus far are consistent with the strategic directions being promoted by the Chamber both in respect of trade and investment liberalization in general and Latin America in particular.

Trade talks are somewhat analogous to playing tennis in a fog. You're not quite sure where the ball is being hit or how hard. So let me try to cut through the mist and provide you this morning with a "Coles Notes" version of a Canadian business response to the theme of your Summit—namely, "What should happen from a trade perspective within the Hemisphere through to the end of this decade and into the next century?"

This represents basically a five part answer:

To begin with, Canadian business will willingly participate in the movement to open trade and investment relations in the Hemisphere in a manner and at a pace that will ensure long-term stability, sustained growth and economic benefit to all parties. We see the setting of pragmatic and achievable objectives for trade liberalization in

Timothy Page is Senior Vice President, International, Canadian Chamber of Commerce.

the Hemisphere as consistent with and complementary to our multilateral efforts through the GATT/WTO.

It is also clear that not all economies in the Hemisphere are at the same level of development nor that they all share a common vision of how they wish to develop. And, frankly there is no real understanding within the Canadian business community of the speed at which the people of Latin America are able or willing to adapt to the domestic changes that will be occasioned by opening their economies to barrier-free trade and investment. Change can be a tough pill to swallow if a country's citizens don't believe open markets to be essential to the long-term prosperity and vitality of their economies.

We know this from direct experience as our business and labor force and governments adjust to the implementation of the Canada-U.S. FTA, the NAFTA and the soon to be implemented Uruguay Round of the GATT. These realities should not be underestimated as policy makers contemplate the pace of moving to hemispheric free trade.

We also know as a trade dependent country, however, with roughly 30 percent of our GNP generated from trade outside of our own domestic borders, that future growth in our economy and maintenance of our standard of living are dependent on our pursuit of market share in this global village.

Second Answer. Canadian business strongly endorses NAFTA as the vehicle of preference within Hemisphere to extend to other Hemisphere partners, over time, the rights and responsibilities currently enjoyed by Mexico, the U.S. and Canada. To expand trade and investment liberalizing objectives through a succession of bilateral agreements would only produce a confusing, complex, and trade distorting operating environment for business.

To date, NAFTA has proven to provide a strong stimulus to trade among all parties. For instance, since NAFTA, Canada's trade with Mexico has increased by 40 percent and Mexican imports to Canada are up by 41 percent. Chile seems well-positioned to become the first South American economy to join the NAFTA family.

Third Answer. To hasten and improve the prospects of other economies joining NAFTA, the following should be emphasized: the importance of ongoing domestic reforms in Latin America which will make of each country a more receptive, stable, transparent, predictable rules-based and market-oriented environment within which to conduct business. This is particularly important for small and medium-sized businesses who usually don't have the resources to work their way around barriers.

We should also be encouraging the establishment of bilateral investment protection agreements, double taxation agreements and perhaps intellectual property accords. We can also conclude understandings related to greater standardization of customs procedures, facilitation of business travel and government procurement access—and movement towards complementarity of national standards, testing and certification procedures. These are all practical, business-oriented stepping stones to enhance commercial interaction amongst Hemispheric partners.

Fourth Answer. As Latin America grows, Canadian business will be there offering its goods, services, technologies and expertise. I am thinking particularly of the power generation industry, the oil and gas and mining sectors, telecommunications, infrastructure development industries, transportation and environmental technologies. With 4 percent annual growth rates projected in Latin America and given the very small amount of trade from Canada to the region currently, (2 percent of total exports and $2.5 billion FDI), the future holds great promises in Latin America for Canadian enterprises. The Prime Minister's visit to South America in January 1995 will no doubt raise excitement and awareness about these opportunities for Canadian companies.

Fifth Answer. I would be remiss in providing this synopsis of the Canadian business community's positive appetite for trade liberalization in Latin America, if I did not remind you of the importance we attach to our bilateral relationship with the United States. We know that we must diversify our export markets. Our support of opening markets in Asia through APEC and the GATT and our interest, as an organization, in promoting Latin America are indications of where we hope Canadians can become more directly involved.

However, 80 percent of our current exports are to the U.S. and there remains unfinished business from the Canada-U.S. and NAFTA agreements, particularly as they relate to trade remedy laws.

Therefore, we believe that efforts to broaden free trade in the Hemisphere must be in a manner that is complementary to Canada's continuing efforts to deepen the integration of the North American market, and not a substitute for it.

By way of conclusion, let me say that the Canadian Chamber is busily preparing our businesses, particularly the small and medium-sized enterprises, to be ready for the international arena. We are also very interested in focusing our members' attention on the opportunities available to them in Latin American markets. In this respect we need to help to foster a much better mutual understanding of our economies, our cultures, our traditions and social an political environments.

As the national Chamber in Canada, we are interested in establishing contact with national chambers from the Hemisphere to increase awareness and begin dialogue to understand how we might support each other, and in the process assist our business members.

As a case in point, we have helped to establish an annual forum for national chambers from Mexico, the U.S. and Canada for entrepreneurs and local chambers to meet to exchange business opportunities.

Our fourth Trilateral meeting is scheduled for the end of March '95 in Houston, Texas.